Understanding
Dispensationalists

Understanding Dispensationalists

Second Edition
With Postscript

Vern S. Poythress

PUBLISHING
P.O. BOX 817 • PHILLIPSBURG • NEW JERSEY 08865

To My Wife Diane

Copyright © 1987 by Vern Sheridan Poythress
Second edition 1994

All Scripture quotations, unless otherwise noted, are taken from the *Holy Bible: New International Version* (North American Edition), copyright © 1973, 1978, 1984 by the International Bible Society, used by permission of Zondervan Bible Publishers.

Printed in the United States of America.

Library of Congress Cataloging-in-Publication Data

Poythress, Vern S.
    Understanding dispensationalists / Vern S. Poythress. –2nd ed.
        p.   cm.
    Includes bibliographical references.
    ISBN 0-87552-374-9
    1. Dispensationalism—Controversial literature. 2. Covenant theology. I. Title.
BT157.P68 1994
230'.046—dc20   93-39295

CONTENTS

ACKNOWLEDGMENTS

This book is dedicated to my wife, Diane, in gratitude for her encouragement and support.

I am indebted to Westminster Theological Seminary for granting me a sabbatical in the fall of 1983 to conduct research for this book. I have also received invaluable help from Bruce Waltke and from many Westminster Seminary students with backgrounds in or concerns for dispensationalism.

I am grateful for the many constructive suggestions that I have received from dispensationalists and for the hospitality that I received from the faculty of Dallas Theological Seminary during my study there. I am most grateful that in our day many dispensationalists and covenant theologians alike are showing themselves willing to lay aside past biases and acknowledge some of the insights that exist on the other side.

1
GETTING DISPENSATIONALISTS AND NONDISPENSATIONALISTS TO LISTEN TO EACH OTHER

Numerous books have been written in an attempt to show that dispensationalism is either right or wrong. Those books have their place. The Bibliography has a sampling of them. In this book, however, I intend to take a different approach, exploring the ways that can be found to have profitable dialogue and to advance our understanding. I believe dialogue is possible in principle even between "hardline" representatives of dispensational theology and equally "hardline" representatives of its principal rival, covenant theology. Until now hardline representatives have been tempted to regard the opposing camp as unenlightened. To some the opposing views seemed so obviously in error that it was easy to find fault with the opponents or even to cease to talk with them. In this book we will attempt to shed light on this conflict.

In the dispute between dispensationalism and covenant theology, both sides cannot be right. It might be that one position is right and the other wrong. Or it might be that one position is mostly right but still has something to learn from the opposing position. So it is important to seriously listen to more than one point of view to ensure that some significant truths have not been overlooked.

If, after our investigation, we conclude that people in one position are basically mistaken, that still does not mean that every aspect or concern of their theology is in error. Still less does it mean that we cannot learn something from the people involved. As individuals they are important, and more is at stake than simply making up our minds about a theological

7

position. We also need to wrestle with the question of how best to communicate with those who differ with us and to sympathize with them where we genuinely can.

I am not a dispensationalist in the classical sense of the word. But precisely for that reason I find it appropriate to spend some time examining dispensationalism in detail, trying to understand the concerns of those who hold that position. I will not spend equal time looking at its chief rival, covenant theology. To do so would take another book. But I will briefly look at some current developments in covenant theology to assess whether there are opportunities for rapprochement and growth in mutual understanding between these opposing positions.

In a word, we will be trying to understand other people, not just make up our minds. At the same time we can never ignore the concern for truth. The questions raised by dispensationalism and covenant theology are important ones. We must all make decisions about what the Bible's teaching really is. That is one reason why some people write vigorous polemics in an attempt to extol the virtues of their position.

Rather than assuming complete familiarity with dispensationalism on the part of my readers and jumping into the middle of the discussion, I will begin by surveying some of the past and present forms of dispensationalism (chapters 2–3). I will also note some recent moves made by covenant theologians that bring them closer to a modified dispensationalism (chapter 4). Readers who are already quite familiar with the present state of affairs may wish to begin at chapter 7, where the focus is more on advancing the discussion beyond its present state.

Since covenant theology and dispensationalism both include a spectrum of positions, not everything I say will apply to everyone. Many covenant theologians and many modified dispensationalists have already adopted a good deal of the material in chapters 11–13, but many can still profit, I hope, from a more thorough assimilation of the ideas in those chapters.

Let us begin by taking a look at dispensationalism in its historical origins and its present-day forms, a subject that dispensationalists are naturally interested in, and one that ought to interest nondispensationalists too. The latter need to try to understand sympathetically—not necessarily to agree, but to understand.

THE TERM "DISPENSATIONALIST"

What do we mean by "dispensationalist"? The term is used by dispensationalists themselves in more than one way. Variations in its use have caused confusion. For the sake of clarity, let us consider a new but completely neutral designation: D-theologians. By D-theologians I mean those who, in addition to a general evangelical theology, hold to the bulk of distinctives characteristic of the prophetic systems of J. N. Darby and C. I. Scofield. Representative D-theologians include Lewis Sperry Chafer, Charles L. Feinberg, Arno C. Gaebelein, J. Dwight Pentecost, Charles C. Ryrie, and John F. Walvoord. These people have, here and there, some significant theological differences. But for most purposes any one of them might serve as a standard for the group. What these men primarily have in common is a particular view of the parallel-but-separate roles and destinies of Israel and the church. Accompanying this view is a particular hermeneutical stance in which careful distinction is made between what is addressed to Israel and what is addressed to the church. What is addressed to Israel is "earthly" in character and is to be interpreted "literally."[1]

D-theologians have most often been called "dispensationalists" because they divide the course of history into a number of distinct epochs. During each of these epochs, God works out a particular phase of his overall plan. Each particular phase represents a "dispensation" in which there are distinctive ways that God exercises his government over the world and tests human obedience.

However, the word "dispensationalist" is not really apt for labeling the D-theologians. Virtually all ages of the church and all branches of the church have believed that there are distinctive dispensations in God's government of the world, though sometimes the consciousness of such distinctions has grown

---

[1] I realize that such a description may strike many D-theologians as inaccurate. They would want to characterize their approach to interpreting *all* parts of the Bible as uniformly literal. But, as we shall see, such was not the way Darby and Scofield described their own approach. While Darby and Scofield affirmed the importance of literal interpretation, they also allowed symbolic (nonliteral) interpretation with respect to the church. Of course, in our own modern descriptions we are free to use the word "literal" in a different way than did Darby or Scofield. But then the word "literal" is used in a less familiar way, and such a use has serious problems of its own (see chapters 8 and 9).

dim. The recognition of distinctions between different epochs is by no means unique to D-theologians.

The problem is compounded by the fact that some D-theologians have used the word "dispensationalist" in both a broad sense and a narrow sense. In the broad sense a "dispensationalist" is anyone who acknowledges that there are distinctive epochs in God's government of the world. Thus according to Feinberg (p. 69; quoted from Chafer, *Dispensationalism*, p. 9):

> (1) Any person is a dispensationalist who trusts the blood of Christ rather than bringing an animal sacrifice. (2) Any person is a dispensationalist who disclaims any right or title to the land which God covenanted to Israel for an everlasting inheritance. And (3) any person is a dispensationalist who observes the first day of the week rather than the seventh.

This is indeed a broad use of the term. On the other hand, at other points D-theologians use the term narrowly to describe *only* their own group, the people whom we have called D-theologians. For example, directly after Feinberg's quote above, he continues: "The validity of that [Chafer's] position is amply attested when the antidispensationalist Hamilton sets forth three dispensations in his scheme: (1) pre-Mosaic; (2) Mosaic; and (3) New Testament."

Hamilton is called an "antidispensationalist" even though he meets Chafer's broad criteria for being a "dispensationalist." Thus "antidispensationalist" is on occasion conveniently used in a narrow sense with reference to those who are in opposition to D-theologians. This shifting of terminology is unhelpful (see Fuller, *Gospel and Law,* p. 10).

One of the effects of having two senses for the term is to engender some lack of precision, or at least lack of clear communication, in discussing church history. Some D-theologians have at times minimized the novelty of D-theology by pointing to the many points in church history where distinctions between epochs have been recognized (cf., e.g., Feinberg, pp. 67–82; Ryrie, *Dispensationalism Today,* pp. 65–74). For one thing they have regarded all premillennialists as their predecessors. All premillennialists recognize that the Millennium is an epoch distinct from both this age and the eternal state. And generally speaking they also recognize the widely held distinctions between pre-Fall and post-Fall situations, and between

Old Testament and New Testament. Hence all premillennialists believe in distinctive redemptive epochs or dispensations. As such they have been viewed as precursors to D-theologians. But, using such an idea of dispensations, we can range even further afield. For example Arnold D. Ehlert includes Jonathan Edwards (and many others like him) in *A Bibliographic History of Dispensationalism*. Edwards, however, was a postmillennialist and a covenant theologian. By most he would be classified as inhabiting the camp diametrically opposed to D-theology. Because he showed particular sensitivity to the topic of redemptive epochs in his book *The History of Redemption*, Edwards has been included in Ehlert's bibliography. Similar reasoning has led to the inclusion of others not normally considered to be dispensationalists.

In reality, then, belief in dispensations (redemptive epochs or epochs in God's dominion) as such has very little to do with the distinctiveness of the characteristic forms of D-theologians (see Radmacher, pp. 163–64). Then why has the subject come up at all? D-theologians do have some distinctive things to say about the content and meaning of particular dispensations, especially those of the church age and the Millennium. The salient point is what the D-theologians say about these dispensations, not the fact that they exist.

Therefore Ehlert's, Feinberg's, and Ryrie's observations about church history, though true, are largely beside the point. They do not constitute an answer to people who have argued that D-theology is a novelty in church history. Let us make an analogy. Suppose you had charged a group of people with teaching a novelty on the topic of *sin*. What would you think if, in reply, they showed the many similarities that their position had with the past on the topic of Christ's resurrection as a solution to sin? Something analogous to this has actually happened. Opponents charge that D-theology is novel in its basic tenet that Israel and the church have parallel-but-separate roles and destinies. Some D-theologians reply by pointing to the fact that the idea of dispensations is not novel.

It is unfortunate that the discussions have not proceeded on a higher level. I encourage my D-theologian brothers to make a good case for the long history of the idea that Israel and the church have parallel-but-separate roles and destinies, if such a case can be made. They should not shift the ground in the discussion by maneuvering with the term "dispensationalist." If a historical case *cannot* be made, they should stand for the truth as something discovered relatively recently. They can still say that their truth was vaguely sensed in the age-long consciousness of the church, consciousness that it is not simply a straight-line continuation of Israel.

Let us return, however, to the main point. The debate is not over whether there are dispensations. Of course there are! Nor is the debate over the number of dispensations. People can make almost as many as they wish by introducing finer distinctions. Hence, properly speaking, "dispensationalism" is an inaccurate and confusing label for the distinctiveness of D-theologians; but some specific terminology is needed. For the sake of clarity, their distinctive theology might perhaps be called "Darbyism" (after its first proponent), "dual destination-ism" (after one of its principal tenets concerning the separate destinies of Israel and the church), or "addressee bifurcation-ism" (after the principle of hermeneutical separation between meaning for Israel and significance for the church).[2] History, however, has supplied the terms "dispensationalism" and "dispensationalist."

Today the theological picture is still more complex. Many contemporary dispensationalist scholars have now modified considerably the classic form of D-theology (see the discussion in chapter 3). They do not hold that Israel and the church are two peoples of God with two parallel destinies. Nor do they practice hermeneutical separation between distinct addressees. They still wish, however, to be called dispensationalists. They do so not only because their past training was in classic dispensationalism, but because they maintain that Israel is still a unique national and ethnic group in the sight of God (Rom. 11:28–29). National Israel is still expected to enjoy the fulfillment of the Abrahamic promises of the land in the millennial period. Moreover they believe in common with classic dispensationalism that the rapture of the church out of the world will precede the Great Tribulation described in Matthew 24:21–31 and the Book of Revelation.

[2]It should be noted that Feinberg sees covenant theology as having the "dual hermeneutics" (p. 79). Since both dispensationalism and covenant theology must deal with the distinctions between epochs of God's dominion, each is bound to have certain theological distinctions and dualities. Those dualities flow over into the area of hermeneutics. What matters is the *kind* of dualities that we are talking about. My terminology is intended to capture the distinctive duality of dispensationalist hermeneutics, without being evaluative or pejorative.

In our day, therefore, we are confronted with a complex spectrum of beliefs. No labeling system will capture everything. For the sake of convenience, I propose to use the term "classic dispensationalism" to describe the theology of D-theologians and "modified dispensationalism" for those who believe in a single people of God but still wish to be called dispensationalists. The boundary lines here, however, are vague. There is a whole spectrum of possible positions bridging the gap between classic dispensationalism on the one side and nondispensational premillennialism on the other side.

THE HISTORICAL FORM OF THE BIBLE

Everyone must reckon with the historical form of the Bible. Since it was written over the course of a number of centuries, not all of the Bible applies to us or speaks to us in the same way. How do we now appreciate the sacrificial system of Leviticus? How do we understand our relation to the temple at Jerusalem and the Old Testament kings? These things have now passed away. A decisive transition took place in the death and resurrection of Christ. What kind of transition was this?

Moreover, a transition of a less dramatic kind already began in the events narrated in the Gospels. John the Baptist announced, "Repent, for the kingdom of heaven is near" (Matt. 3:2). A crisis came at the time of John's appearing. What sort of change of God's relation to Israel and to all people does this crisis involve? No serious reader of the Bible can avoid these questions for long. And they are difficult questions, because they involve appreciating elements of both continuity and discontinuity. There is only one God and one way of salvation (continuity). But the coming of Christ involves a break with the past, a disruption and alteration of existing forms (discontinuity).

Ethical questions also arise. If some elements in the Bible do not bear directly on us, what do we take as our ethical norms? How far are commands and patterns of behavior in the Old Testament, in the Gospels, or in Acts valid for us? What commands are still binding? How far do we imitate examples in the Bible? If some things are not to be practiced, how do we avoid rejecting everything?

These questions are made more difficult whenever Christian theology deemphasizes history. Dispensational distinctives arose for the first time in the nineteenth century, in a time when much orthodox theology, and particularly systematic theology, did not bring to the fore enough the historical and progressive character of biblical revelation. Systematic theology, in its concern with what the Bible as a whole says on any particular topic, may neglect the diversity and dynamic character of God's Word coming to different ages and epochs. Dispensationalism arose partly in an endeavor to deal with those differences and diversities in epochs. It endeavored to bring into a coherent, intelligible relationship differences that might otherwise seem to be tensions or even contradictions within the Word of God itself.

Others have told the story of the development of dispensationalism more thoroughly than I can (see Fuller, *Hermeneutics;* Bass, Dollar, Marsden). It is not necessary to rehearse their accounts. But we should note two other concerns dispensationalism responded to even at the beginning. Dispensationalism arose as an affirmation of the purity of salvation by *grace* and as a renewal of fervent expectation for the second coming of Christ. These concerns are both evident in a powerful way in the life of John Darby, the first proponent of the most salient distinctives of dispensationalism. Thus Darby is important, not merely as a founder of dispensationalism, but as a representative of some of the elements that continue to be strong concerns of dispensationalists to this day.

JOHN NELSON DARBY (1800–82)

Darby's life manifests a dual concern for purity in his own personal life and purity in the life of the church as a community. A decisive transition, a "deliverance," occurred in his personal life during a time of incapacitation because of a leg injury. Darby describes this in a letter (*Letters,* 3:298):

> During my solitude, conflicting thoughts increased; but much exercise of soul had the effect of causing the scriptures to gain complete ascendancy over me. I had always owned them to be the word of God.
>
> When I came to understand that I was united to Christ in heaven [Eph. 2:6], and that, consequently, my place before God was represented by His own, I was forced to the conclusion that it was no longer a question with God of

this wretched "I" which had wearied me during six or seven years, in presence of the requirements of the law.

Darby thus came to appreciate much more deeply the grace of God to sinners and the sufficiency of the work of Christ as the foundation for our assurance and peace with God. A person may well be shaken to the roots by such an experience. Darby had obtained the true purity, the true righteousness, not that which comes from the law (Phil. 3:9).

In close connection with this, Darby's view of the church and of corporate purity also underwent a transformation. In the next sentence of the same letter, Darby continues (*Letters,* 3:298):

> It then became clear to me that the church of God, as He considers it, was composed only of those who were so united to Christ [Eph. 2:6], whereas Christendom, as seen externally, was really the world, and could not be considered as the "church."

As the backside of his appreciation of the exalted character of Christ and of union with Christ, Darby came to a very negative evaluation of the visible church of his day. There was some justification for his conclusion. James Grant (p. 5; quoted in Bass, p. 73) indicates the low and unspiritual character of the church life of Darby's day:

> Men's minds were much unsettled on religious subjects, and many of the best men in the Church of England had left, and were leaving it, because of the all but total absence of spiritual life, blended with no small amount of unsound teaching, in it. The result was, that many spiritually minded people ... were in a condition to embrace doctrines and principles of Church government, which they considered to be more spiritual than were those which were then in the ascendency in the Establishment.

Darby built his view of the church directly on his christology, and there was a great appeal and attractiveness to his view. The true church, united to Christ, is heavenly. It has nothing to do with the existing state of earthly corruption.

Darby joined a church renewal movement, later called the Plymouth Brethren, that had a desire for purification similar to his own. He soon became one of its principal leaders. His contribution may have started with a zeal for Christ, but it ended with an indiscriminate rejection of everyone out of conformity with Darby's ideas: "He [God] has told us when the church was become utterly corrupt, as He declared it would do, we were to turn away from all this corruption and those who were in it, and turn to the scriptures" (Darby, *Writings,* 20:240–41 [*Ecclesiastical Writings,* no. 4, "God, Not the Church"]; quoted by Bass, p. 106). From there Darby ended up saying that only the Brethren meet in Christ's name (Bass, pp. 108–9). Restoration of the corrupt church is impossible because the dispensation is running down (ibid.). Excommunication operated against some Plymouth Brethren who disagreed with Darby.

Darby's distinctive ideas in eschatology appear to have originated from his understanding of union with Christ, as did his views of the church. He says (*Letters,* 3:299): "The consciousness of my union with Christ had given me the present heavenly portion of the glory, whereas this chapter [Isa. 32] clearly sets forth the corresponding earthly part."

Both the heavenly character of Christ and the reality of salvation by grace apart from works of the law made Darby feel an overwhelming distance between his own situation of union with Christ and the situation of Israel discussed in Isaiah 32. Israel and the church are as different as heaven and earth, law and grace. It is a powerful appeal, is it not? Of course both Darby and present-day dispensationalists emphasize that they intend to build their doctrines on the Bible, not merely on a theological inference. But this is compatible with saying that the theological inference has a valuable confirmatory influence. Though present-day dispensationalists may differ from Darby here and there, the same appeal remains among them to this day.

Unfortunately Darby did not realize that the distance and difference he perceived could be interpreted in more than one way. Darby construed the difference as primarily a "vertical," static distinction between heaven and earth and between two peoples inhabiting the two realms. He did not entertain the possibility that the difference was primarily a historical one, a "horizontal" one, between the language of promise, couched in earthly typological terms, and the language of fulfillment, couched in terms of final reality, the reality of God's presence, the coming of heaven to human beings in Jesus Christ. Darby was reacting against a dehistoricized understanding of the Bible that had little appreciation for the differences between redemptive epochs.

In my judgment, however, Darby did not wholly escape from the problems that he reacted against. He still did not reckon enough with the magnitude of the changes involved in the historical progression from promise to fulfillment. Hence he was forced into an untenable "vertical" dualism between the parallel destinies of two parallel peoples of God. But we are getting ahead of ourselves. What is important to notice at this point is the desire of Darby to do full justice to a difference that he saw, a difference that is actually there in the Bible. He wanted to do justice to the importance of Ephesians 2:6 for eschatology and our understanding of Israel.

Out of Darby's understanding of Ephesians 2 (and other passages) arose a rigid distinction between the church and Israel. The church is heavenly, Israel earthly. Darby says (*Writings,* 2:373): "The great combat [of Christ and Satan] may take place either for the earthly things . . . and then it is in the Jews; or for the church . . . and then it is in the heavenly places."

From this follows a dichotomous approach to interpretation or hermeneutics. Darby says (ibid., 2:35):

> First, in prophecy, when the Jewish church or nation (exclusive of the Gentile parenthesis in their history) is concerned, i.e., when the address is directed to the Jews, there we may look for a plain and direct testimony, because earthly things were the Jews' proper portion. And, on the contrary, where the address is to the Gentiles, i.e., when the Gentiles are concerned in it, there we may look for symbol, because earthly things were not their portion, and the system of revelation must to them be symbolical. When therefore facts are addressed to the Jewish church as a subsisting body, as to what concerns themselves, I look for a plain, common sense, literal statement, as to a people with whom God had *direct* dealing upon earth.

One final quote may illustrate the close connection in Darby's mind between christology, concern for purity in the church, and hermeneutical bifurcation (Darby, *Writings,* 2:376):

> Prophecy applies itself properly to the earth; its object is not heaven. It was about things that were to happen on the

earth; and the not seeing this has misled the church. We
have thought that we ourselves had within us the accomplishment of these earthly blessings, whereas we are called
to enjoy heavenly blessings. The privilege of the church is
to have its portion in the heavenly places; and later
blessings will be shed forth upon the earthly people. The
church is something altogether apart—a kind of heavenly
economy, during the rejection of the earthly people, who
are put aside on account of their sins, and driven out
among the nations, out of the midst of which nations God
chooses a people for the enjoyment of heavenly glory with
Jesus Himself. The Lord, having been rejected by the
Jewish people, is become wholly a heavenly person. This is
the doctrine which we peculiarly find in the writings of the
apostle Paul. It is no longer the Messiah of the Jews, but a
Christ exalted, glorified; and it is for want of taking hold of
this exhilarating truth, that the church has become so
weak.

In Darby, then, we see bound up with one another (1) a
sharp distinction between law and grace; (2) the sharp vertical
distinction between "earthly" and "heavenly" peoples of God,
Israel and the church; (3) a principle of "literal" interpretation
of prophecy tying fulfillment up with the earthly level, the
Jews; (4) a consequent strong premillennial emphasis looking
forward to the time of this fulfillment; (5) a negative, separatist
evaluation of the existing institutional church. The premillennial emphasis (4) was the main point of entrance through which
Darby's distinctives gained ground in the United States. But all
the other emphases except (5), the separatist emphasis, soon
characterized American dispensationalism. The separatist emphasis gained ground in the United States only later, around
1920–30, as fundamentalism lost hope of controlling the
mainstream of American denominations (see Marsden).

2
CHARACTERISTICS OF SCOFIELD DISPENSATIONALISM

What happened to dispensational teaching after Darby's time? Dispensationalism came to the United States partly through a number of trips by John Darby to the United States, partly through literature written by Darby and other Plymouth Brethren. Dispensationalism spread through the influence of prophetic conferences in the late nineteenth and early twentieth centuries. Fuller (*Hermeneutics*, pp. 92–93) argues that dispensationalism took root in the United States more on the basis of its eschatological teaching than on the basis of Darby's concept of Israel and the church as two peoples of God:

> It appears, then, that America was attracted more by Darby's idea of an any-moment Coming than they [*sic*] were by his foundational concept of the two peoples of God. . . . Postmillennialism made the event of the millennium the great object of hope; but Darby, by his insistence on the possibility of Christ's coming at any moment, made Christ Himself, totally apart from any event, the great object of hope. Darby was accepted [in America] because, as is so often the case, those revolting from one extreme took the alternative presented by the other extreme.

Notice that once again christology was the deep ground for the attractiveness of dispensationalism.

Within this movement the Scofield Reference Bible, in particular, contributed more than any other single work to the spread of dispensationalism in the United States. Because of its widespread use, it has now in effect become a standard. Hence we need first to come to grips with its teachings. Afterwards we can talk about ways in which these teachings are modified by other dispensationalists. Dispensationalism is now a diverse movement, so that not everything characteristic of the Scofield approach ought to be attributed to all dispensationalists.

GENERAL DOCTRINES OF C. I. SCOFIELD

Cyrus I. Scofield (1843–1921) was indebted to James Brookes and Brethren writings for many of the views that he held in common with John Darby. What views does Scofield offer us in the notes of his reference Bible? First of all, Scofield's teachings and notes are evangelical. They are mildly Calvinistic in that they maintain a high view of God's sovereignty. Scofield affirms the eternal security of believers and the existence of unconditional promises. Moreover his emphasis on the divine plan for all history would naturally harmonize with a high view of God's sovereignty.

What elements distinguish Scofield from other Evangelicals? There are four main focuses of difference. First, Scofield practices a "literal" approach to interpreting the Bible. This area is complicated enough to warrant a separate section for discussion (pp. 22–27).

Second, Scofield sharply distinguishes Israel and the church as two peoples of God, each with its own purpose and destiny. One is earthly, the other heavenly. For example, the Scofield Reference Bible note on Genesis 15:18 says:

(1) "I will make of thee a great nation." Fulfilled in a threefold way: (a) In a natural posterity—"as the dust of the *earth*" (Gen. 13.16; John 8.37), viz., the Hebrew people. (b) In a spiritual posterity—"look now toward *heaven* . . . so shall thy seed be" (John 8.39; Rom. 4.16,17; 9.7,8; Gal. 3.6,7,29), viz. all men of faith, whether Jew or Gentile. (c) Fulfilled also through Ishmael (Gen. 17,18–20)[*sic*; Gen. 17:18–20 is intended].

The note on Romans 11:1 reads:

The Christian is of the heavenly seed of Abraham (Gen. 15.5,6; Gal. 3.29), and partakes of the spiritual blessings of the Abrahamic Covenant (Gen. 15.18, *note*); but Israel as a nation always has its own place, and is yet to have its greatest exaltation as the earthly people of God.

Chafer, a writer representing a view close to Scofield's, states the idea of two parallel destinies in uncompromising form ("Dispensationalism," p. 448):

> The dispensationalist believes that throughout the ages God is pursuing two distinctive purposes: one related to the earth with earthly people and earthly objectives involved, while the other is related to heaven with heavenly people and heavenly objectives involved. Why should this belief be deemed so incredible in the light of the facts that there is a present distinction between earth and heaven which is preserved even after both are made new; when the Scriptures so designate an earthly people who go on as such into eternity; and an heavenly people who also abide in their heavenly calling forever? Over against this, the partial dispensationalist, though dimly observing a few obvious distinctions, bases his interpretation on the supposition that God is doing but one thing, namely the general separation of the good from the bad, and, in spite of all the confusion this limited theory creates, contends that the earthly people merge into the heavenly people.

A third point of distinctiveness is the precise scheme for dividing the history of the world into epochs or dispensations. The Scofield note on Ephesians 1:10 speaks of dispensations as "the ordered ages which condition human life on the earth." In Scofield's notes there are seven in all (cf. note on Gen. 1:28):

Innocency (Eden; Gen. 1:28)
Conscience (Fall to Flood; Gen. 3:23)
Human Government (Noah to Babel; Gen. 8:21)
Promise (Abraham to Egypt; Gen. 12:1)
Law (Moses to John the Baptist; Exod. 19:8)
Grace (church age; John 1:17)
Kingdom (millennium; Eph. 1:10)

Of course people who are nondispensationalists might well accept that these were seven distinct ages, and might even say that the labels were appropriate for singling out a prominent feature of God's dealings with human beings during each age. As already noted (pp. 9–13), the mere belief in dispensations does not distinguish dispensationalism from many other views. Scofield's distinctiveness comes into view only if we ask what Scofield believes *in detail* about God's ways with human beings during each of these dispensations. At this point some of the distinctiveness is a matter of degree. Scofield may emphasize more sharply the discontinuities between dispensations. But the most outstanding point of difference lies in Scofield's views concerning the church age in relation to the Millennium. During the church age God's program for earthly Israel is put to one side. It is then taken up again when the church is raptured. The time of the church is a "parenthesis" with respect to earthly Israel, a parenthesis about which prophecy is silent (because prophecy speaks concerning *Israel's* future). One can see, then, that Scofield's view concerning the *kind* of distinctiveness the dispensations possess is a reflection of his view concerning Israel and the church.

A fourth and final point of distinctiveness is the belief in a pretribulational rapture. According to Scofield the second coming of Christ has two phases. In the first, the "Rapture," Christ comes to remove the church from the earth. But he does not appear visibly to all people. After this follows a seven-year period of tribulation. At the end of seven years, Christ appears visibly to judge the nations, and the earth is renewed (see diagram 2.1, taken from Jensen, p. 134).

Though this is one of the best known aspects of popular dispensationalism, it is not as foundational as the other distinctives. It is simply a product of the other distinctives. Nevertheless it is an important product. Scofield maintains that the church and Israel have distinct, parallel destinies. Since prophecy concerns Israel and not the church, the church must be removed from the scene at the Rapture *before* Old Testament prophecy can begin to be fulfilled again. At that time Israel will be restored and Daniel 9:24–27 can run to completion. If the church is not removed, the destinies of the church and Israel threaten to mix. Thus the theory of parallel destinies virtually requires a two-phase Second Coming, but the two-phase Second Coming does not, in itself, necessarily imply the theory of parallel destinies.

SCOFIELD'S HERMENEUTICS

Dispensationalists are often characterized as having a literal hermeneutics. But in the case of Scofield, this is only a half truth. The more fundamental element in Scofield's approach is his distinction between Israel and the church. In a manner

Diagram 2.1

The World's Last Two Battles

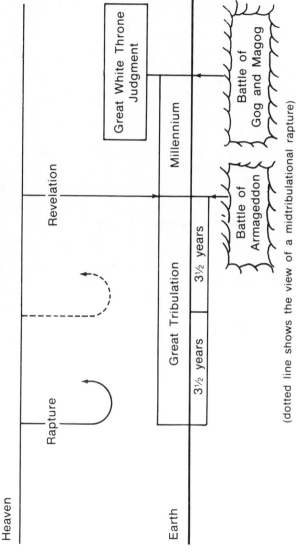

(dotted line shows the view of a midtribulational rapture)

From *Jensen Bible Study Charts* by Irving L. Jensen. Copyright 1976, 1980 Moody Press. Moody Bible Institute of Chicago. Used by permission.

reminiscent of Darby, Scofield derives from this bifurcation of two peoples of God a bifurcation in hermeneutics. Israel is earthly, the church heavenly. One is natural, the other spiritual. What pertains to Israel is to be interpreted in literalistic fashion. But what pertains to the church need not be so interpreted. And some passages of Scripture—perhaps a good many—are to be interpreted on both levels simultaneously. In the *Scofield Bible Correspondence School* (pp. 45–46), Scofield himself says:

> These [historical Scriptures] are (1) literally true. The events recorded occurred. And yet (2) they have (perhaps more often than we suspect) an *allegorical* or *spiritual* significance. Example, the history of Isaac and Ishmael. Gal. iv. 23–31. . . .
>
> It is then permitted—while holding firmly the historical verity—reverently to *spiritualize* the historical Scriptures. . . .
>
> [In prophetic Scriptures] we reach the ground of *absolute literalness.* Figures are often found in the prophecies, but the figure invariably has a literal fulfillment. Not one instance exists of a "spiritual" or figurative fulfillment of prophecy. . . .
>
> Jerusalem is always Jerusalem, Israel always Israel, Zion always Zion. . . .
>
> Prophecies may never be spiritualized, but are always literal.

Scofield is a not a pure literalist, but a literalist with respect to what pertains to Israel. The dualism of Israel and the church is, in fact, the deeper dualism determining when and where the hermeneutical dualism of "literal" and "spiritual" is applied.[1]

---

[1] For specific examples of Scofield's spiritualization of historical Scriptures, see the notes in the Scofield Reference Bible on Genesis 1:16; 24:1; 37:2; 41:45; 43:34; Exodus 2:2; 15:25; 25:1, 30; 26:15, introduction to Ruth; John 12:24. Ezekiel 2:1 can also be included as an instance of spiritualization based on a historical part of a prophetic book. The introductory note to Song of Solomon should also be noted.

Many present-day dispensationalists would see Scofield's examples of spiritualization as "applications" rather than interpretations that give the actual meaning of a passage. To view spiritualization as application is certainly possible, but it is not quite the same as Scofield's approach. One may have "applications" of still future prophecies as well as past history (for example, there are many present practical applications of the doctrine of the Second Coming). Hence the meaning/application distinction does not have the same effect as the history/prophecy distinction that Scofield introduces.

CHARACTERISTICS OF SCOFIELD DISPENSATIONALISM

Scofield does insist that both historical and prophetic Scriptures have a literal side. The historical passages describe what literally took place in the past, while the prophetic passages describe what will literally take place in the future. He rejects any attempt to eliminate this literal side. But would he allow a spiritual side in addition? If so, we would expect him to say that both historical and prophetic Scriptures are to be interpreted literally as to the actual happenings described, and spiritually as regards any application to the church. This is not what he says. Instead he introduces a distinction between prophecy and history.

Even this bifurcation, however, is not the complete story. Scofield wanders from his own principle with respect to "absolute literalness" of prophecy in the note on Zechariah 10:1. The passage itself reads, "Ask ye of the LORD rain in the time of the latter rain: so the LORD shall make bright clouds, and give them showers of rain, to every one grass in the field" (KJV). The note says, "Cf. Hos. 6.3; Joel 2.23–32; Zech. 12.10. There is both a physical and spiritual meaning: Rain as of old will be restored to Palestine, but, also, there will be a mighty effusion of the Spirit upon restored Israel." Hence this "ground of absolute literalness" in prophecy is not so absolute as we might suppose. Scofield is willing not only to recognize figures but to speak of double meanings. The one thing that must be excluded is not a "spiritual" meaning but an interpretation that would imply that the church participates in the fulfillment of this prophecy.

To a nondispensationalist this procedure might seem to be highly arbitrary. But it does not seem so to Scofield. The procedure is in fact based on a certain understanding of Ephesians 3:3–6. Classic dispensationalists usually understand the passage to be teaching that the Old Testament does not anywhere reveal knowledge of the New Testament church. Nevertheless the idea of "mystery" in Ephesians 3 does allow that the church could be spoken of covertly, as in typology. What is not allowed is an *overt* mention of the church. If Old Testament prophecy, as prophecy of the future, mentioned the church, it would have been a matter of overt prediction. Old Testament historical accounts, on the other hand, might have a second "mystery" level of meaning available to the New Testament readers.

Such an understanding of Ephesians 3:3–6, then, helps

justify a hermeneutical approach like Scofield's. But of course that is not the only possible interpretation of Ephesians 3:3–6. This passage says that the *way* in which Gentiles were to receive blessing, namely by being incorporated into Christ on an equal basis with Jews (v. 6), was never made clear in the Old Testament. The claim that the mystery in Ephesians 3:3–5 was not previously revealed need mean no more than that.

Scofield's hermeneutics is beautifully illustrated by precisely those cases where one might suppose that literalism would get into trouble. Here and there the New Testament has statements that, on the surface, appear to be about fulfillment of Old Testament promises and prophecies. And some of these fulfillments turn out to be nonliteral. But Scofield rescues himself easily by distinguishing two levels of meaning, a physical-material (Israelitish) and a spiritual (churchly).

As a first example, take the promises in Genesis concerning Abraham's offspring. Galatians 3:8–9, 16–19, 29 appear to locate fulfillment in Christ and in Christ's (spiritual) offspring. Scofield's note on Genesis 15:18 neatly defuses this problem by arguing that there are two parallel offsprings, physical and spiritual, earthly and heavenly. Hence fulfillment in the spiritual offspring is not *the* fulfillment Israel waits for.

Next look at Matthew 5–7. The Sermon on the Mount speaks of fulfillment of the law (5:17). This fulfillment appears to involve fulfillment not only in Christ's preaching, but in the disciples of Christ whose righteousness is to exceed the righteousness of the scribes and Pharisees (5:20; cf. v. 48). These disciples, and especially the Twelve, as salt and light (5:13–16), form the nucleus of the church (16:18). Hence Matthew 5–7, including the promises of the kingdom of heaven, pertains to the church. But Scofield finds that the same route of explanation is available. The Scofield note on 5:2 says, "The Sermon on the Mount has a twofold application: (1) Literally to the kingdom. In this sense it gives the divine constitution for the righteous government of the earth. . . . (2) But there is a beautiful moral application to the Christian. It always remains true that the poor in spirit, rather than the proud, are blessed."

Again, in Acts 2:17 Peter appears to say that Joel 2:28–32 (a prophecy with respect to Israel) is being fulfilled in the *church* events of Pentecost. Scofield's note on Acts 2:17 boldly invokes a distinction:

A distinction must be observed between "the last days" when the prediction relates to Israel, and the "last days" when the prediction relates to the church (1 Tim. 4.1–3; 2 Tim. 3.1–8; Heb. 1.1,2; 1 Pet. 1.4,5; 2 Pet. 3.1–9; 1 John 2.18,19; Jude 17–19). . . . The "last days" as related to the church began with the advent of Christ (Heb. 1.2), but have special reference to the time of declension and apostasy at the end of this age (2 Tim. 3.1; 4.4). The "last days" as related to Israel are the days of Israel's exaltation and blessing, and are synonymous with the kingdom-age (Isa. 2.2–4; Mic. 4:1–7).

Scofield's general principle of "absolute literalism" with respect to prophetic interpretation would seem to lead us to say that Joel is referring to Israel and *not* the church. But since Peter is using the passage with reference to the church, Scofield has to make room for it. He does so by splitting the meaning in two. On one level it refers to Israel, but on a secondary level it can still refer to the "last days" of the church. And that is apparently what Scofield does in his note on Joel 2:28:

"Afterward" in Joel 2:28 means "in the last days" (Gr. *eschatos*), and has a partial and continuous fulfilment during the "last days" which began with the first advent of Christ (Heb. 1.2); but the greater fulfilment awaits the "last days" as applied to Israel.

In several instances, then, Scofield postulates two separate meanings for the same passage, one Israelitish and the other churchly. To retain the primacy of the Israelitish "literal" fulfillment, the churchly reference may be spoken of as an "application" (note, Matt. 5:2) or a "partial . . . fulfilment" (note, Joel 2:28). This method is summarized in diagram 2.2.

ELABORATIONS OF SCOFIELD'S DISTINCTIONS

The introduction of distinctions remains a favorite method among classic dispensationalists for resolving difficulties. Scofield, for example, distinguishes the kingdom of God from the kingdom of heaven in no less than five aspects (Scofield note on Matt. 6:33). Most nondispensationalist interpreters, by contrast, see the two phrases as simply translation variants of *malkut shamaim* (cf. Ridderbos, *Kingdom,* p. 19). Again, with premillennialists generally, Scofield introduces a distinction between two last judgments in his note on Matthew 25:32, and between two separate battles of Gog and Magog (note on Ezek. 38:2).

Diagram 2.2

Bifurcation Into Earthly and Heavenly Meaning

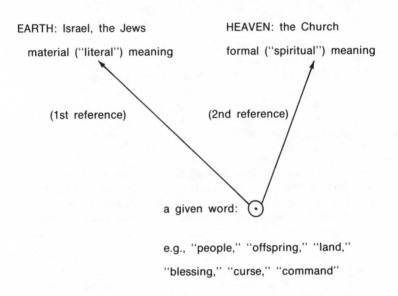

To preserve intact the Israel/church distinction, Scofield distinguishes also between the wife of Jehovah and the bride of the Lamb (note on Hos. 2:1):

> Israel is, then, to be the restored and forgiven wife of Jehovah, the Church the virgin wife of the Lamb (John 3.29; Rev. 19.6–8); Israel Jehovah's earthly wife (Hos. 2.23); the Church the Lamb's heavenly bride (Rev. 19.7).

The practice of postulating two levels of meaning to a single passage (such as Scofield does with Matt. 5:2 and Joel 2:28) also occurs with other dispensationalists. For instance Tan (p. 185) distinguishes two comings of "Elijah" related to the text of Malachi 4:5. John the Baptist "foreshadowed" and "typified" the coming of Elijah predicted in Malachi 4:5. But, if the principle of literalness is to be protected, John cannot actually *be* the fulfillment. Elijah the Tishbite will come in a future literal fulfillment. Tan is quite explicit about the hermeneutical principle involved in making such distinctions:

> It is possible of course to see present foreshadowings of certain yet-future prophecies and to make applications to the Christian church. But we are here in the area of "expanded typology." Premillennial interpreters may see a lot of types in Old Testament events and institutions, but they see them as applications and foreshadowments—not as actual fulfillments. (p. 180)

> Literal prophetic interpreters believe that citations made by New Testament writers from the Old Testament Scriptures are made for purposes of illustrating and applying truths and principles as well as pointing out actual fulfillments. (p. 194)

Hence we should be aware that many Old Testament prophecies can be related to the church in terms of "application." But there are variations here in the way in which different dispensationalists deal with this relation. Since the relation of Old Testament prophecy to the church is a key point in the dispute, we will look at the variations in dispensationalism in detail in the next chapter.

3
VARIATIONS OF DISPENSATIONALISM

For both J. N. Darby and C. I. Scofield, the interpretation of law and prophecy—virtually the whole Old Testament—had a key role in the dispensational system. Law, such as occurs in the Sermon on the Mount, cannot directly bear on the Christian, lest the truth of salvation by grace be compromised. Prophecy is to be read in terms of literal fulfillment in a future earthly Israel, not in the church. These still remain key factors in the approach of some dispensationalists. But it must not be imagined that everyone's approach to Old Testament law and prophecy is exactly the same.

USE OF THE OLD TESTAMENT IN PRESENT-DAY APPLICATIONS

It is important, for one thing, to recognize a distinction between different dispensationalist practices in the application of the Bible to people's lives. Many contemporary dispensationalists read the Bible as a book that speaks directly to themselves. They read prophetic promises (e.g., Isa. 65:24; Jer. 31:12–13; Ezek. 34:24–31; Joel 2:23; Mic. 4:9–10) as applicable to themselves. They apply the Sermon on the Mount to themselves. They do this even if they believe that the primary reference of such prophecies and commands is to the Millennium. Included in this group are many classic dispensationalists as well as those who have significantly modified dispensational theology in some way.

There are, however, some dispensationalists who refuse to

do this kind of application. They engage in "rightly dividing the word of truth."[1] That is, they carefully separate the parts of the Bible that address the different dispensations. People following this route learn that the Sermon on the Mount is "legal ground" (cf. Scofield's note on Matt. 6:12). It is kingdom ethics, not ethics for the Christian. Christians are not supposed to pray the Lord's Prayer (Matt. 6:9–13), or use it as a model, because of the supposed antithesis to grace in 6:12. These dispensationalists might be called "hardline" dispensationalists. The opposite group might be called "applicatory" dispensationalists, because they regularly make applications of the Old Testament to Christians. We will find some classic dispensationalists in both groups.

Some hardline dispensationalists hold to such principles without even qualifying them to the degree that Scofield does in the note on Matthew 5:2. (Scofield speaks of "a beautiful moral application to the Christian" after he has made his main point about the fact that Matthew 5–7 refers to the millennial kingdom.) Moreover, when hardline dispensationalists read prophecy, they divide that which is millennial from that which is fulfilled in the first coming. Through this process, without always realizing it, they carefully refrain from applying almost anything to themselves as members of the church.

Of course the differences among dispensationalists in the application of the Bible to themselves are a matter of degree. One can apply to oneself a greater or lesser number of passages to a greater or lesser degree. Nevertheless the distinction I am making is useful because it helps us to evaluate more accurately how serious the differences are.

Dispensationalists and nondispensationalists both think that the other side is in error. But what net effect does the controversy have on the church? In terms of the practical effects, applicatory dispensationalists and most nondispensationalists are closer to each other than either one is to hardline dispensationalists.

Let us see how the effects work out. Consider first the applicatory dispensationalists and nondispensationalists to-

[1] I do not intend to criticize the expression itself (it is biblical: 2 Tim. 2:15 KJV). Neither am I criticizing attempts to distinguish addressees of prophecy. I am concerned here for the practice of forbidding applications on the basis of a division.

gether. One of these two groups has some erroneous ideas about the details of eschatological events. Such errors are bound to affect their lives to a certain extent. All Christians are called on to live their lives in the light of their hope for Christ's coming. And our hopes are always colored to some degree by the detailed pictures that we have in our minds. Nevertheless the details do not have much effect in comparison with the central hope, which we all share. Many of the details are just details sitting on the shelf, without much effect one way or the other on our lives. If they are proved wrong when the events actually take place, it is no great tragedy. If there is a problem here, it is less with the detailed eschatological views than with erroneous practical conclusions drawn from them. For instance, people who believe that the political state of Israel will be vindicated in the tribulation period may erroneously conclude that their own government should *now* side with the Israeli state in all circumstances. Or because they believe that the coming of the Lord is near, they may abandon their normal occupations, in a manner similar to what some of the Thessalonians did (2 Thess. 3:6–13). But these are abuses that mature dispensationalists and nondispensationalists alike abhor.

Now consider the hardline dispensationalists, those who do not apply large sections of the Bible to themselves. If they are wrong, the damage they are doing is very serious. They are depriving themselves of the nourishment and discipline that Christians ought to receive from many portions of the Bible. When they are in positions of prominence, they damage others also. They are distancing themselves from promises and commands that they ought to take seriously. They are undercutting the ability of the Word of God to come home to people's lives as God intended. Clearly not all the promises and the commands in the Bible apply to us in exactly the same way that they applied to the original hearers. Many times we must wrestle with the question of how the Word of God comes to bear on us. But simply to eliminate that bearing is to short-circuit the process. It is a potentially dangerous way out.

What can we learn from this variation within dispensationalism? Those of us who are not dispensationalists can learn not to condemn or react against dispensationalists indiscriminately. Some dispensationalists are much closer to us spiritually than are others. Some are teaching destructively; others are not. Particularly when we pay attention to the practical pay-offs of

32

dispensationalists' teachings and the way that dispensationalists are nourished by the Bible, we must recognize that matters are complex. Some dispensationalists are doing many things that nondispensationalists would approve of. The differences that remain may, in practice, be more minor than what they look like in theory.

It is important that those who are applicatory dispensationalists deal with this major difference in *practice* among dispensationalists. Applicatory dispensationalists are, I believe, already doing a good job in applying Old Testament prophecy practically and pastorally. But they need to help others out of errors here. And applicatory dispensationalists should recognize that some nondispensationalists are closer to them in their practical use of the Bible than are the hardline dispensationalists.

SOME DEVELOPMENTS BEYOND SCOFIELD

Some interesting developments have occurred among dispensationalists that take us significantly beyond the views of Scofield himself. The *New Scofield Reference Bible* stands substantially in the tradition of Scofield. But in a few respects, at least, some more controversial elements of Scofield's teaching have been removed. For example the notes on Genesis 15:18 and Matthew 5:2 setting forth the twofold interpretation of Abrahamic promise and kingdom law have disappeared. But the twofold approach to Acts 2:17 remains, and is possibly even strengthened in the new edition. The new edition adds material at Genesis 1:28 stressing that there is only one way of salvation: salvation is in Christ, by grace, through faith. The same editorial note also stresses the cumulative character of revelation. The dispensations, of course, are still there; but they are seen as adding to earlier works of God rather than simply superseding them. Both of these emphases are welcome over against earlier extreme positions (see Fuller, *Gospel and Law*, pp. 18–46).

In addition there is an important development of a more informal kind. I see increasing willingness among some leading dispensationalists to speak at least of secondary applications or even fulfillments of some Old Testament prophecy in the church. Many would say that New Testament believers participate in fulfillment by virtue of their union with Christ, the true Seed of Abraham. Remember that Scofield altogether rejected this type of move in his general statement about the "absolute literalness" of Old Testament prophecy (Scofield, *Scofield Bible Correspondence School,* pp. 45–46). But that left Scofield with an extremely uncomfortable tension between his hermeneutical principle and some of his practice, which allowed a spiritual, churchly dimension to the promise to Abraham, to the Joel prophecy, and to Matthew's kingdom ethics. Moreover, the insistence on literalness alone in prophecy grated against Scofield's willingness to see allegorical elements in Old Testament history. Why was an extra dimension allowed for history (which on the surface contained *fewer* figurative elements) and disallowed for prophecy (which on the surface contained *more* figurative elements)? It was inevitable that some of Scofield's successors would try to remove the stark and artificial-sounding dichotomy that Scofield had placed between history and prophecy.

The way to remove the dichotomy between history and prophecy is simple. One adds to Scofield the possibility that prophecy may, here and there, have an extra dimension of meaning, parallel to the extra dimension found in Old Testament history. What sort of extra dimension is this? For history one preserves the genuine historical value of the account while adding to it, in some cases, a typological dimension pointing to Christ and the church. For prophecy one preserves the literal fulfillment in the millennial kingdom of Israel while adding to it, in some cases, a dimension of spiritual application pointing to Christ and the church. Some would go even further and speak of the church's participation in fulfillment.

The dispensationalist Tan, for example, though quite careful to insist on completely literal fulfillments of prophecy, is quite willing to acknowledge an area of application to the church. He speaks (p. 180) of "present foreshadowings" of the fulfillment:

> It is possible of course to see present foreshadowings of certain yet-future prophecies and to make applications to the Christian church. But we are here in the area of "expanded typology." Premillennial interpreters may see a lot of types in Old Testament events and institutions, but they see them as applications and foreshadowments—not as actual fulfillments.

Scofield had, of course, recognized the existence of typology and even "allegory" in Old Testament historical accounts. But on the level of principle, he refused to do this in the area of prophecy. Tan has no such reservation.

Tan, however, is careful to preserve an important distinction in his terminology. He consistently uses the word "fulfillment" to designate the coming to pass of predictions in their most literal form (most often millennial fulfillment is in view). "Foreshadowing" and "application" are preferred terms for the way prophecies may relate to the church. But other dispensational interpreters go even further. Erich Sauer (*Eternity*, pp. 162–78) is willing to speak of the possibility of fourfold fulfillment of many Old Testament prophecies. They are fulfilled (1) in a preliminary way in the restoration from Babylon, (2) further (spiritually) in the church age, (3) literally in the Millennium, and (4) finally in the consummation (the eternal state following the Millennium).

Sauer is explicit about his point of view. One might wonder whether others leave the door open for a similar point of view by postulating the possibility of multiple fulfillments. Irving Jensen (p. 132) speaks for much of popular dispensationalism:

> Often one prophecy had a multiple application—for example, a prophecy of tribulation for Israel could refer to Babylonian captivity as well as the Tribulation in the end times.
>
> . . . A prophet predicted events one after another (mountain peak after mountain peak), as though no centuries of time intervened between them. Such intervening events were not revealed to him.

The idea of multiple application easily arises as one attempts to deal with the obvious parallels between Old Testament prophecies and some of the events associated with the first and second comings of Christ. Moreover the examples in which the New Testament applies the Old Testament to Christians open the way for recognition that the church and Christians are often one important point of application. Suppose that dispensationalists come to Old Testament prophecies with an expectation that the prophecies will frequently have multiple applications. As Christian preachers, because of their audience and their location in history, they have a special

Diagram 3.1

The Nature of Fulfillment

A. C.I. Scofield

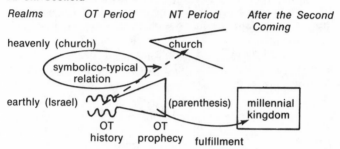

B. Modified Dispensationalism

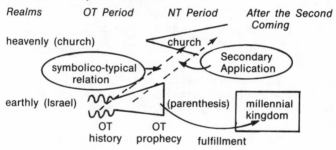

C. One-People-of-God Dispensationalism

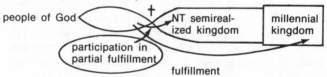

D. Preconsummationism ("amil")

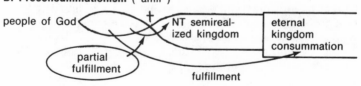

obligation to pay attention to any applications to the church. Of course they will do well to investigate in a preliminary way what the ultimate fulfillment is and what applications there are to people in situations other than their own. But if they have a pastoral heart, they will devote much effort and time to the question of present-day application. As they do this, their own approach to prophetic interpretation will draw closer to that of nondispensationalists.

In fact, we can plot a whole spectrum of possible positions here (see diagram 3.1). Dispensationalists may start by talking in terms of applications. But as they become more comfortable with the connection between prophecies and the church, they call such applications preliminary or partial fulfillments. In part such a change is simply a difference in terminology. But the word "fulfillment" tends to connote that the use of the passages by the church is not so far away from their main meaning. It suggests that when God gave the prophecies in the first place, the church was not merely an afterthought but integral to his intention.

In fact, dispensationalists sometimes shift even further. More and more prophecies are seen as being fulfilled both in the church age (in a preliminary way) and in the millennial age (in a final way). But if so, the church is not so alien to Israel's prophetic heritage. Rather the church participates in it (in a preliminary way). Christians participate now in the fulfillment of Abrahamic promises, because they are in union with Christ who is the heart of the fulfillment. The full realization of the promises, however, still comes in the future. Hence there are not two parallel sets of promises, one for Israel and one for the church. There are no longer parallel destinies, one for Israel and one for the church. Rather there are different historical phases (preliminary and final) of one set of promises and purposes. And therefore there is really only one people of God, which in latter days, after the time of Christ's resurrection, incorporates both Jew and Gentile in one body (cf. the single olive tree in Rom. 11:16–32).

At this point dispensationalists come to a position close to classic premillennialism, like that of George E. Ladd. Classic premillennialism believes in a distinctive period of great earthly prosperity under Christ's rule after his bodily return. Following this period there is a general resurrection and a creation of new heavens and a new earth (the consummation or eternal state).

But it does not distinguish two peoples of God or two parallel destinies. Some dispensationalist scholars agree with this view. They still call themselves dispensationalists because they wish to emphasize the continuing importance of national, ethnic Israel (Rom. 11:28–29). They expect that the Abrahamic promises concerning the land of Palestine are yet to find a literal fulfillment in ethnic Israel in the millennial period.

If we wish, we can imagine a transition all the way into an amillennial position. Suppose that some classic premillennialists, as time passes, see more and deeper fulfillments of Old Testament prophecy in the church age. A fulfillment still deeper than what they see cannot easily stop short of being an absolute, consummate fulfillment. All along they have viewed the greater fulfillment as taking place in the Millennium. But now they may begin to believe that this "millennial" peace and prosperity is so good that it goes on forever. It is in fact the consummation of all things. Of course they will now have to revise their view of Revelation 20:1–10. There are several options for the way this revision might happen. These options need not concern us. The major point is that perceptions about Old Testament prophecy can range over a very broad continuum. We can hope that other brethren will approach us along this continuum, even if some of them never reach a point where they consciously abandon a whole system in order to absorb another whole system at once. Dispensationalists may revise their position into one like classic premillennialism or even amillennialism. Conversely amillennialists may become premillennialists by introducing an extra threshold stage into the beginning of what they have termed the eternal state. It is possible for people to revise their system piecemeal and still arrive in the end where we are. (Or, vice versa, we can find ourselves revising our views until we arrive where they are.)

As long as we are in this life, there will be some doctrinal disagreements among Christians. But for the sake of Christ and for the sake of the truth, we must work toward overcoming them (Eph. 4:11–16). And on this issue we need not despair just because people do not come to full agreement right away.

4
DEVELOPMENTS IN COVENANT THEOLOGY

It is time to look at the developments outside dispensationalism, particularly developments in covenant theology, which has long been considered the principal rival to dispensationalism.

Even though historically covenant theology has been a rival, it is not necessarily an antithetical twin to classic dispensationalism. An alternative position may not always claim to have as many detailed and specific views of prophetic interpretation as classic dispensationalism. Not all views of prophecy lend themselves equally well to precise calculations about fulfillment. Some prophetic language may be allusive or suggestive, rather than spelling out all its implications. Hence we may sometimes have to take a long time to work out the details of how fulfillment takes place. Any genuine alternative position nevertheless still shares a firm conviction of the truth of the doctrines of Evangelicalism: the inerrancy of the Bible, the deity of Christ, the Virgin Birth, the substitutionary atonement of Christ, the bodily resurrection of Christ, etc.

In the previous chapters we asked those who were nondispensationalists to try to understand someone else's position. So now we may equally ask dispensationalists to try to understand another position. You may not agree, but understand that there is a real alternative here, and understand that it makes sense when viewed sympathetically "from inside," just as your system makes sense when viewed sympathetically "from inside."

We will not attempt to discuss covenant theology in depth but confine our survey to some of the principal features.

MODIFICATIONS IN COVENANT THEOLOGY

Covenant theology had its origins in the Reformation and was systematized by Herman Witsius and Johannes Cocceius. For our purposes we may pass over a long history of origins and start with classic covenant theology, as represented by the Westminster Confession of Faith. Covenant theology organizes the history of the world in terms of covenants. It maintains that all God's relations to human beings are to be understood in terms of two covenants, the covenant of works made with Adam before the Fall, and the covenant of grace, made through Christ with all who are to believe. The covenant of grace was administered differently in the different dispensations (Westminster Confession 7.4) but is substantially the same in all.

Covenant theology has always allowed for a diversity of administration of the one covenant of grace. This diversity accounted in large part for the diversity of epochs in biblical history. But the emphasis was undeniably on the unity of *one* covenant of grace. By contrast classic dispensationalism began with the diversity of God's administration in various epochs and brought in only subordinately its affirmations of the unity of one way of salvation in Jesus Christ.

What has happened since? Covenant theologians have not simply stood still with the Westminster Confession. Geerhardus Vos began a program of examining the progressive character of God's revelation and the progressive character of God's redemptive action in history. Vos's reflection has issued in a whole movement of "biblical theology," emphasizing much more the discontinuities and advances not only between Old Testament and New Testament, but between successive epochs within the Old Testament. Among its representatives we may mention Herman Ridderbos, Richard B. Gaffin, Meredith G. Kline, and O. Palmer Robertson. Within the discipline of biblical theology each particular divine covenant within the Old Testament can be examined in its uniqueness, as well as in its connection to other covenants. Covenant theologians within this framework still believe in the unity of a single covenant of grace. But what does this unity amount to? The single "covenant of grace" is the proclamation, in varied forms, of the single way of salvation. Dispensationalists do not really disagree with this unity!

In addition there have been movements on other fronts.

Anthony A. Hoekema's book *The Bible and the Future* enlivens the area of eschatology by emphasizing the biblical promise of a new earth. He is an amillennialist; but by emphasizing the "earthy" character of the eternal state (the consummation), he produces a picture not too far distant from the premillennialist's Millennium.

Finally Willem Van Gemeren reflects about the special role of Israel on the basis of Romans 11 and Old Testament prophecy. By allowing for a future purpose of God for ethnic Israel, he again touches on some of the concerns of dispensationalists.

A VIEW OF REDEMPTIVE EPOCHS OR DISPENSATIONS

Let us try to summarize the results of this work that will be most valuable for dispensationalists. First there are distinct epochs or dispensations in the working out of God's plan for history. The epochs are organically related to one another, like the relation of seed to shoot to full-grown plant to fruit. Between epochs there is both continuity (like one tree developing through all its stages) and discontinuity (the seed looks very different from the shoot, and the shoot very different from the fruit). Just how many epochs one distinguishes is not important. What is important is to be ready for an organic type of relationship.

For example, one should be alert to figurative resurrections in the Old Testament: Noah's being saved through the Flood (the water being a symbol of death; cf. Jonah 2:2–6); Isaac's salvation from death by the substitute of a ram; Moses' salvation as an infant from the water; the people of Israel's salvation at the Passover and at the Red Sea; the restoration from Babylon as a kind of preliminary "resurrection" of Israel from the dead (Ezek. 37). All these show some kind of continuity with the great act of redemption, the resurrection of Christ. But they also show discontinuity. Most of them are somehow figurative or shadowy. Even a close parallel like that of Elijah's raising a dead boy is not fully parallel. The boy returned to his earthly existence and eventually died again. Christ is alive forever in his resurrection body (1 Cor. 15:46–49).

The discontinuity is very important. Before the actual

41

appearing of Christ in the flesh, redemption must of necessity partake of a partial, shadowy, "inadequate" character, because it must point forward rather than locating any ultimate sufficiency in itself. Moreover, the particular way in which the resurrection motif is expressed always harmonizes with the particular stage of "growth" of the organically unfolding process. For instance, at the time of Noah, mankind still existed undifferentiated into nations. Appropriately the "resurrection" of Noah's family manifests cosmic scope (2 Peter 3:5–7). At the time of Isaac, the promised offspring and heir of Abraham existed in one person. Appropriately the sacrifice and "resurrection" involves this one as representative of the entire promise and its eventual fulfillment (cf. Gal. 3:16). And so on with the rest of the instances. Each brings into prominence a particular aspect of the climactic work of Christ. It does so in a manner that just suits the particular epoch and particular circumstances in which the events occur.

REPRESENTATIVE HEADSHIP

The unity in this historical development is the unity inherent in God's work to restore and renew the human race and the cosmos. We know that the human race is a unity represented by Adam as head (Rom. 5:12–21). When Adam fell, the whole human race was affected. The creation itself was subjected to futility (Rom. 8:18–25). Redemption and recreation therefore also take place by way of a representative head, a new human head, namely the incarnate Christ (1 Cor. 15:45–49). As there is one humanity united under Adam through the flesh, so there is one new humanity united under Christ through the Spirit. Just as the subhuman creation was affected by Adam's fall (Rom. 8:20), so it is to be transformed by Christ's resurrection (v. 21). Christ himself, as head and representative of all the redeemed, is the unifying center of God's acts of redemption and recreation.

In particular Christ's redemption reconciles human beings both to God and to one another. When we are reconciled to God, we are reconciled to fellow human beings who are also reconciled to God. For example, we learn to forgive one another (Eph. 4:32; Col. 3:13). The redemption that Christ brings transforms both the human individual and the human group. We become children of God, related to one another like members of a family (1 Tim. 5:1). Christ recreates us (Eph. 4:24), bringing us into a new human community, the people of God (Eph. 2:19). There can only be one people belonging to God, because there is only one Christ. Obviously this oneness works in a different way before the Incarnation and the Resurrection. It can have only a preliminary and shadowy form until Christ's work is actually accomplished. But we cannot think of the Old Testament people of God as a second people of God alongside the New Testament people of God. These are two successive historical phases of the manifestation of the corporate and community implications of Christ's representative headship.

It is not fully relevant when some dispensationalists bring in the topic of God's dealings with the angels. They say, "If God has separate purposes for angels, well then, he may have separate purposes for Israel and the church." But the angels were never united under Adam's headship. They did not fall with Adam; neither are they redeemed from their sins by being united to Christ by faith. Hence the destiny of the angels does not confront us with the same types of questions. When it comes to human redemption, Romans 5:12–21 shows us the way we must think. It excludes in principle the idea of two parallel peoples of God, because the corporate unity of the people of God derives from their common representative Head.

DICHOTOMY AT THE CROSS OF CHRIST

In the light of dispensationalist concern for diversity and discontinuity between historical epochs, it is particularly necessary to reckon with the radical break in history that took place in the life of Christ, above all in his death, resurrection, and ascension. There is a dichotomy here, a dichotomy of "before" and "after." Christ's work made a real and lasting difference. God's relation to human beings can never be the same afterwards because now redemption has been accomplished. There is, then, a very great distinction between Israel and the church. But the distinction is basically a historical one, not a metaphysical one. It is the distinction between before and after Christ's resurrection, not a distinction between heavenly and earthly.

True, Christ is the Man from *heaven* (1 Cor. 15:47–49). Our citizenship is in heaven (Phil. 3:20). But this is because heaven is the throne of God, the starting point and model for renewal of the whole cosmos. We must not construe heaven simply as a static otherness, but as a power source that will transform the whole. Moreover the heaven–earth contrast is not now a contrast between what is ethereal and vaporous, on the one hand, and what is physical and solid on the other. Christ's own resurrection body is quite real, quite tangible (Luke 24:39). We might say that it is *the* really real, since Christ is to remain permanently while all other physical things are transformed (2 Peter 3:10–12).

Also we ought not to vaporize or overly individualize the kind of fulfillment of Old Testament promises that we experience in union with Jesus Christ. Christ is Lord of our *bodies,* Lord of the *community* of God's people, not simply Lord of the individual soul.

A number of questions, however, remain. Does this mean that the Jews as such, from Pentecost onward, have lost every kind of distinctive status over against the Gentiles? No. If you have once been a member of God's people, you are "marked for life" (cf. Rom. 11:29). You are in a different position than if you had never been in this kind of relationship with God. You are more grievously responsible if you apostasize (2 Peter 2:21–22).

Romans 11 tells the story very effectively. Some dispensationalists construe the olive tree in Romans 11 as a symbol for being in the place of spiritual opportunity and privilege. It certainly involves such opportunity. But it also implies being holy (Rom. 11:16). To be part of the olive tree is thus similar to being part of the "holy nation" of 1 Peter 2:9. It is similar to what Peter means by being "a chosen people, . . . a people belonging to God" (1 Peter 2:9). Some Jews have been cut off from their place in the olive tree so that Gentiles might be grafted in; but Jews in their cutting off remain cultivated olive branches, and they can be grafted in again. This is quite consistent with the fact that there is only one holy (cultivated) olive tree, hence one people of God, and one root. Salvation comes to cut-off Jews precisely as they are reunited to the olive tree, as they renew their status as part of the people of God, as they receive again fellowship with God, as they receive nourishment from the root.

Why are the two separate terms "Israel" and "the church" usually used for Jews and the church in the New Testament?

Superficially this might seem to point to the idea of two parallel peoples of God. But one must remember that theology is not to be deduced directly from vocabulary stock (cf. Barr, Silva). In fact, the New Testament usage is rather complex, since many instances of the use of "Israel" refer to the people of God before the transition that took place at the resurrection of Christ and Pentecost. Some uses are quotations from the Old Testament. But beyond this several terms are needed in a complex situation where some of the Old Testament people of God have been cut off from their fellowship with God (Rom. 11). The obvious and convenient decision to use "Israel" and "the Jews" (*hoi Ioudaioi*) most of the time to designate the Jewish people need not entail any denial of the deeper conceptual and theological unity between Old Testament and New Testament phases of existence of one people of God (cf. 1 Peter 2:9–10).

More generally, all interpreters need to recognize that the Bible is written in everyday and sometimes literary language, not technically precise language of later systematicians. We must allow that the meanings of individual words are not infinitely precise, and that the particular sense that a word has is codetermined by its immediate context (cf. Barr, Silva).

UNDERSTANDING BY OLD TESTAMENT HEARERS

Next, what about the Old Testament recipients of prophecy? Did they understand what they were being told? How did they understand it? These questions need more detailed discussion later (see chapter 9). For the moment let me say that I believe that the Old Testament hearers understood. But they need not have understood as precisely or as fully as we can in the light of seeing the fulfillment in Jesus Christ. They understood sufficiently well to be nourished and encouraged in their time. For example, as they listened to Isaiah's prophecies of a new exodus (cf., e.g., Isa. 51:9–11), they would have realized that it was figurative: they need not return to Egypt, cross miraculously through the Red Sea, and wander again in the wilderness in order to experience it. What exact literal form it would take was left open-ended. They might not be sure exactly which details were figurative, and in exactly which respects they were figurative. But they knew what the substance of it was: a deliverance as mighty and all-embracing as the first exodus.

If things, however, are sometimes left vague like this description in Isaiah, how do we control our understanding of Scripture in general and of prophecy in particular? Again these are questions that one could spend a long time answering. Basically the answers can be summed up in a few words.

1. We use grammatical-historical interpretation. That is, we ask what the passage meant in the historical and linguistic situation in which it was originally recorded.
2. We use Scripture to interpret Scripture. Clear passages can sometimes help us with more obscure ones. When fulfillments actually come, they help us to understand the prophecies more fully.
3. Main points are clearer than details. We can be sure of the main points even at times when we are not confident that we have pinned down all the details. Things that the Bible teaches in many places or with great emphasis are held with greater confidence than things taught once or in passing (because we are not so sure that we have understood the details correctly).
4. We may rightly expect cumulative fulfillment of many prophecies that envision long-range promises or threats. Willis J. Beecher has expounded this matter ably:

In the nature of things a promise, operative without limit of time, may begin to be fulfilled at once, and may also continue being fulfilled through future period after period. (p. 129)

According to one idea a generic prediction is one which regards an event as occurring in a series of parts, separated by intervals, and expresses itself in language that may apply indifferently to the nearest part, or to the remoter parts, or to the whole—in other words, a prediction which, in applying to the whole of a complex event, also applies to some of the parts. (p. 130)

Others speak of the successive or the progressive fulfillment of a prediction. An event is foretold which is to be brought about through previous events that in some particulars resemble it. (p. 130)

THE MILLENNIUM AND THE CONSUMMATION

Now what about the Millennium? What are we to expect in the future? For one thing we expect the coming of Christ. All God's promises are yes and amen in Jesus Christ (2 Cor. 1:20). Moreover, all the promises are relevant to the church; all apply to us in some fashion, directly and indirectly. But not all are fulfilled in the church as such. Some are not at present fulfilled at all in the church. Some are only partially fulfilled in the church. In studying some prophecies we come to think that their full realization is still future. In principle this fuller realization could take place either in the final golden age, the consummation of all things, described in Revelation 21:1–22:5,[1] or in a "silver" age, commonly called "the Millennium," distinct from both the consummation and from the present time. Some prophecies may have their fulfillment in the silver age, others in the golden age, others in both. The language of Revelation 21:1–22:5 indicates that the consummation will be the greatest fulfillment of the bulk of Old Testament prophecy. It will not be an ethereal kingdom but a new heavens and a new *earth,* an earth as physical and solid as Christ's own resurrection body (Hoekema, pp. 274–87; see further chapter 12).

The emphasis on the new earth helps to bring the traditional millennial positions closer to one another. If all are able to agree that the new earth represents the most intensive fulfillment, arguments about fulfillments of a lesser scope will seem to be less crucial. Moreover the emphasis on the new earth represents a definite, salutary advance over all the traditional millennial positions. Most amillennialists, premillennialists, and postmillennialists alike have usually put their greatest emphasis on fulfillment in the millennial period. They have then disagreed among themselves over the character and date of the Millennium. This has been particularly bad for amillennialists, because it leaves them with no emphasis at all on a distinctively "earthy" character to fulfillment. Dispensationalists have rightly objected to this kind of "spiritualization" (Hoekema, pp. 205, 275; quoting Walvoord, *Millennial Kingdom,* pp. 100–102, 298).

It is surpassingly important, then, to include in our reckoning the new earth of Revelation 21:1–22:5. Even when

---

[1] I realize that some postmillennialists interpret Revelation 21:1–22:5 as referring to the silver age (Millennium). I strongly disagree with this interpretation, but I cannot argue the case in this work.

we do so, we can expect people still to disagree over whether the Bible teaches the existence of a distinctive silver age in the future (Millennium). Some will think that such an age is necessary for the fulfillment of *some* Old Testament prophecies, and that Revelation 20:1–10 teaches the existence of such an age. On the other hand, others will think that the second coming of Christ will bring so sweeping a victory over sin and its consequences that from then on the reign of Christ physically and visibly on earth will continue forever, with no further need to deal with sin. The issue at stake in our present discussion is not how sweeping the consequences of the Second Coming are, how intensive the fulfillment is, but whether the fulfillment at that time will be an organic continuation of what Christ has done now. In this age he has integrated Gentiles and Jews into one body through the cross (Eph. 2:16). Will there be one people of God at that time or not? I say that there will be, because there is only one representative Head who brings them to salvation by uniting them to himself.

One thing more needs to be said about millennial disputes. Some judicious discrimination and sensitivity are needed when we venture to criticize other views for *global* failures. Postmillennialists criticize premillennialists for their pessimism, premillennialists criticize postmillennialists for hopelessly naïve optimism in the face of the world wars. Often such criticisms seem to those in the opposite camp to be caricatures. What looks like a failure when viewed from outside, in terms of a competing system, may very well seem to be a strength when viewed from inside, in terms of the system itself. All millennial views are subject to such problems, since all tend to carry with them a global atmosphere about the course of church history. People tend to read the atmosphere of the opposing system in terms of *their* system, not the opposing system as a whole, and so find it less defensible than it is.

Since we are focusing on dispensationalists, I take my prime example from them. The dispensationalist Charles L. Feinberg (p. 77; quoting Ryrie, "Necessity," p. 44) expresses his view of history as follows:

> Concerning the goal of history, dispensationalists find it in the establishment of the millennial kingdom on earth while the covenant theologian regards it as the eternal state. This is not to say that dispensationalists minimize the glory of the eternal state, but it is to insist that the display must be

seen in the present heavens and earth as well as in the new
heavens and earth. This view of the realization of the goal
of history within time is both optimistic and in accord with
the requirements of the definition. The covenant view,
which sees the course of history continuing the present
struggle between good and evil until terminated by the
beginning of eternity, obviously does not have any goal
within temporal history and is therefore pessimistic.

What do we say about this quotation? Premillennialists in
general are often accused by postmillennialists of being pessimistic, because they postpone the visible triumph of Christ's
kingdom till after his return. But premillennialists themselves
do not see it that way. Feinberg and Ryrie in particular claim to
be truly optimistic. When Feinberg and Ryrie think of the
Second Coming, the associations that they make are different
from those of the postmillennialist. They see the time after the
Second Coming as still having a basic continuity with our
history now. It is the apex of history rather than being simply
beyond our time and therefore leaving our time hopeless. But
because they have no visible triumph within the time span that
the postmillennialist allots for the triumph, it seems *from within
a postmillennialist framework* that they are pessimistic.

Now let us turn to look at Feinberg and Ryrie's criticism of
others. They say that "the covenant view . . . obviously does
not have any goal within temporal history and is therefore
pessimistic." Of course what Feinberg and Ryrie say does not in
fact apply to all covenantal views. It does not apply to
covenantal premillennialism or postmillennialism but only to
amillennialism. Even with respect to amillennialism, their
criticism is skewed. In fact, they make the same mistake with
respect to amillennialism as postmillennialism is tempted to
make concerning premillennialism. From within Ryrie's framework it is obvious that the goal of history, the apex of history,
must arrive within history before the arrival of new heavens and
the new earth. If not, it leaves our time (counted now as
extending up to the end of the old earth) hopeless.

This is not, however, how all amillennialists look at the
matter. For instance, as we have already observed, the amillennialist Hoekema (pp. 274–87) puts special stress on the new
earth. He argues that the consummation in a new heavens and a
new earth is not a totally new beginning but a transformation of
what now is. There is still continuity, just as there is continuity

between Christ's resurrection body and his body before his resurrection.

Hence amillennialists like Hoekema consider that "history" goes on through and beyond the renewal of heaven and earth. They do not think of that final renewal as a distinction between time and eternity (as if there were no sense of time following the renewal). They think of it, not as "starting over from scratch," but as renewal analogous to that of the believer to be a new creation (2 Cor. 5:17). Their vision of the consummation is very like classic premillennialism's vision of the Millennium, except that sin is *entirely* gone. They would say, "We are even more optimistic than the premillennialists about what sort of triumph will take place when Christ returns."

Feinberg and Ryrie, of course, insist that the triumph must be within "temporal history"—but the words "temporal" and "history" have different functions in their dispensationalist system than they do in the above type of amillennialism. Feinberg and Ryrie insist that the triumph must take place before the coming of the new heaven and new earth—but what that new heaven and earth amount to is different for them than for amillennialists. Ryrie argues that dispensationalism is optimistic and amillennialism pessimistic—but only after he has deliberately eliminated the one age about which amillennialists have their most profound optimism. To an amillennialist like Hoekema, Ryrie's criticism must seem like a misunderstanding or a begging of the question.

We may use an analogy. Suppose Ryrie were to propose a competition between his sedan and an amillennialist's pickup truck. Ryrie says, "Let us see which can carry more goods." Ryrie then argues that the sedan can carry more because anything outside the body of the car is not to be counted. For Ryrie adding in the consummation is like putting a luggage rack on the top of the car. That doesn't count in the competition. But for the "earthy" amillennialist, the consummation is like the back of the pickup. It is the purpose for which the whole pickup is made. Of course the amillennialist will lose if one does not allow the use of the back end. Ryrie's argument results in a meaningless victory by fiat.

THE POSSIBILITY OF RAPPROCHEMENT

With only a little exaggeration, one could say that the ideas described above as developments within covenant theology were also developments within dispensational theology. Some of the modified dispensationalists described in chapter 3 hold that there is only one people of God. This affirmation alone brings them into a considerable measure of agreement with the ideas in pages 42–43 above. In fact, some modified dispensationalists agree with the points made in the whole of this chapter. So, provided we are able to treat the question of Israel's relative distinctiveness in the Millennium as a minor problem, no substantial areas of disagreement remain. But not all dispensationalists, nor all covenant theologians for that matter, are in this peaceful position. Therefore we will have to talk about problems that prevent agreement.

5
THE NEAR IMPOSSIBILITY
OF SIMPLE REFUTATIONS

Many Evangelicals who believe that dispensationalism is wrong have discovered that it is not at all easy to *show* this to the satisfaction of dispensationalists. One reason it is difficult to persuade people to change their position is because important issues are involved: many aspects of the relation of the Old Testament to the New depend on one's position concerning dispensationalism.

Classic dispensationalism is a whole system of theology. It has a great deal of internal coherence. A system that is carefully and thoroughly elaborated, whether right *or* wrong, will almost certainly include answers to standard objections; and different parts of the system "come to the aid" of any part that is challenged. To a certain extent such cooperation of the parts takes place in any system of theology. However, generally speaking, it is less true of modified forms of dispensationalism. The modifications noted in chapter 3 have produced "looser" systems allowing more room for each particular text to say something less easily harmonizable with the whole. Hence my observations in this chapter will apply mostly to dispensationalism in its classic form.

HEDGING ON FULFILLMENT

In classic dispensationalism one of the key points of controversy concerns the nature of Old Testament prophecy, in particular the nature of prophetic fulfillment. Are the fulfillments always literal? And what do we mean by "literal"?

The classic dispensationalist claims that all fulfillments in the past have been purely and simply literal. Hence we are to expect the same for prophecies as yet unfulfilled. There are no grounds for doing otherwise. Scofield (*Scofield Bible Correspondence School*, pp. 45–46) says, "Figures are often found in the prophecies, but the figure invariably has a literal fulfillment. Not one instance exists of a 'spiritual' or figurative fulfillment of prophecy."

It is very hard for a nondispensationalist to argue effectively against this claim. The reason is that classic dispensationalists have "hedged" on the idea of fulfillment. They possess an idea of fulfillment and an idea of literalness making it almost impossible *in principle* for the opponent to give a counterexample.

Of course there are some obvious cases of literal fulfillments in the New Testament, which the dispensationalists count as supporting their case. But what happens when a nondispensationalist brings up apparent cases of nonliteral fulfillment, such as Luke 3:5, Acts 2:17–21, Galatians 3:29, and Hebrews 8:8–12? Dispensationalists have several resources at their disposal. For one thing they can claim that the original prophecy had "figures," as Scofield says. Thus Isaiah 40:4 is a figurative prediction of the coming of John the Baptist and does not commit us to expecting topographical changes. But then how do we tell the difference between a figurative and a nonfigurative expression? Is this always perfectly plain to everyone? Dispensationalists have in fact left themselves some convenient maneuvering room. It is possible that sometimes they have decided what is figurative and what is nonfigurative *after* the fact. That is, they may have conveniently arranged their decisions about what is figurative *after* their basic system is in place telling them what can and what cannot be fitted into the system. The decisions as to what is figurative and what way it is figurative may be a product of the system as a whole rather than the inductive basis of it. Or rather we may have a circular process. The needs of consistency with the system help the proponents to decide what is figurative; and making those decisions helps them to produce interpretations of particular texts that support the consistency of the system. Hence we will have to take up in detail at a later point the question of what "literalness" means.

Another route available to dispensationalists is to claim that some apparent nonliteral fulfillments are New Testament "applications" rather than fulfillments. Thus Tan (pp. 193–94) remarks:

> By giving such a broad definition to "fulfillment" [all citations from the Old Testament in the New Testament], nonliteral interpreters clearly prejudice the case in their favor, for such a definition assuredly points to spiritualized fulfillments. It is necessary that this technique be exposed, or attempts at refuting amillennial and postmillennial evidences will have to be on a book-for-book basis.
>
> . . . Literal prophetic interpreters believe that citations made by New Testament writers from the Old Testament Scriptures are made for purposes of illustrating and applying truths and principles as well as pointing out actual fulfillments.

Of course Tan is correct that there are cases of New Testament applications of Old Testament principles, but from this he makes some sweeping conclusions. He thinks it is unnecessary to argue his case about fulfillment "on a book-for-book basis." It looks very much as if he himself holds his position on an a priori rather than a genuinely inductive basis. He has gone to the other extreme and prejudiced the case in favor of literalism. How? Tan (p. 194) maintains that "instances of actual fulfillment are usually introduced in the New Testament by the formula ἵνα πληρωθῇ ('that it might be fulfilled')." He probably does not realize that this restricts the interpreter almost exclusively to the Gospel of Matthew. Only Matthew uses the word "fulfill" regularly in citing the Old Testament. Other New Testament authors, even when they had fulfillment in mind, characteristically used other citation formulas. Hence Tan allows nonliteralists only a very narrow base (Matthew) for their counterarguments. By contrast Tan allows himself to use *every* instance of literal fulfillment in the Bible as evidence for his position.

There is a serious skewing of the evidence here. Apparent nonliteral fulfillments are either (1) counted as literal by pointing to the "figures" in the original prophecy or (2) are said to be applications (not fulfillments). Apparent literal fulfillments are counted as literal. When this process is complete, lo and behold, all fulfillments turn out to be literal. Thus it is concluded that passages still unfulfilled (including those that have been "applied" in a nonliteral way in the New Testament era) will also have a literal fulfillment. Such an argument has a built-in method of excluding counterevidence.

Tan, however, will still have difficulties over the fulfillments in the Gospel of Matthew. These, remember, are not subject to elimination by his procedure, because Matthew quite a few times uses the word "fulfill" in a citation formula. When one understands Matthew's own theology of fulfillment in the entire context of his Gospel, the idea of strict literalness becomes problematic. Nevertheless I do not think that Matthew is a suitable starting point for short discussions with classic dispensationalists. Interpretations of particular texts in Matthew are too much influenced by the global controls of a system (whether dispensationalist or nondispensationalist).

Still one more route is available to dispensationalists to account for apparent nonliteral fulfillments in the New Testament. They can say that the New Testament represents a spiritual level of fulfillment in opposition to the literal level applicable to Israel. This is what Scofield does when he explains the fulfillment of the promise of offspring to Abraham in the church (Gal. 3:29). By such a procedure the level of literal fulfillment to Israel is preserved intact. If such a procedure is used, it is hard to see what kind of evidence from the New Testament could conceivably count against a dispensationalist interpretation of prophecy.

All this means, not that dispensationalism is wrong, but that much of its argumentation concerning the nature of fulfillment is circular. The facility with which dispensationalists answer critics may be due to artificial elimination of counterevidence rather than to having truth on their side.

Critics of dispensationalism can also learn a lesson here. It is generally unwise for them to concentrate their discussion on New Testament texts that speak of fulfillment, for they will only frustrate themselves and their dispensationalist respondents. The more basic issues concern what counts as evidence for fulfillment, and how that fulfillment is itself to be understood. These prior issues largely determine how the dispensationalists or their critics undertake to explain the text and integrate it with their whole system. Since New Testament texts concerning fulfillment usually will not persuade anyone unless these issues are confronted, we should search for better platforms for dialogue.

DISPENSATIONALIST HARMONIZATION

Critics of dispensationalism should also appreciate its remarkable degree of harmoniousness. Every part of dispensationalism harmonizes with almost every other part. If critics attempt to reinterpret a single text in their favor, dispensationalist respondents can often cite two or more other texts that support their own interpretation. Critics soon find themselves called on to reinterpret many, many texts simultaneously.

One element of dispensationalism making this impressive harmony possible is a joint working of two complementary hermeneutical procedures. The first is the multiplying of distinctions. Dispensationalists are willing to introduce some sharp, fine-grained distinctions where almost no one else has seen distinctions. The Rapture, for instance, is distinguished from the second coming of Christ even though, as many dispensationalists acknowledge, there is no consistent terminological difference between the two in the New Testament. The kingdom of God and the kingdom of heaven are distinguished from one another. And so on. (However, many modified dispensationalists no longer hold to as many sharp distinctions. One must be prepared for differences on this point.)

Complementary to this hermeneutical procedure is that of doubling the application of a single expression in a single text of the Bible. Many prophetic texts are thought of as having an earthly fulfillment in Israel and a spiritual application to the church (recall diagram 2.2). Whereas the first procedure splits apart texts that are verbally similar, this procedure joins a single text to two different levels of fulfillment.

It is altogether possible for us to discover, in principle, some distinctions in the Bible that have not been recognized before (the first procedure above). And it is possible for some texts to have more than one fulfillment or application (the second procedure). But one must also recognize that dangers accompany the application of these procedures. If we permit ourselves to invoke both procedures much of the time, we greatly multiply the number of options available for harmonizing different texts of the Bible. We increase enormously the flexibility that we have in interpreting any one text. Hence it becomes relatively easy to harmonize everything *even under the umbrella of an overall system that is not correct*. Dispensationalists rightly feel that the dispensationalist system is in large measure harmonious, stable, and consistent. But this consistency may all too easily be the product of a hermeneutical scheme that is capable of artificially generating consistency by the multiplication of distinctions and the doubling of relationships. Thus in the case of dispensationalism consistency is not a guarantee of truth.

The harmoniousness of dispensationalism stems in large from the backgrounds of its exponents. Darby and Scofield, who both had legal training and were members of the bar, exercised considerable skill in logically harmonizing and arranging a great multitude of texts into a single coherent system. If their scriptural and hermeneutical foundations were correct, so much the better. But if not, they might well have succeeded in producing a very high degree of harmony even on the basis of some false premises. Moreover it must be remembered that their strong point was in logical harmony and contemporary application rather than in grammatical-historical interpretation. Darby's negative attitude to the institutional church virtually cut him off from the fruits of scholarly reflection and interpretation in previous generations of church history.

Contemporary dispensationalists of course have attempted to refine grammatical-historical interpretation within their system. But the attempts at such interpretation within classic dispensationalism are often still too dominated by the presupposition and mind-set of the overall system, a system that remains operative when dispensationalists come to examine particular texts. Grammatical-historical interpretation remains a weak point in classic dispensationalism, as we shall see.

SOCIAL FORCES

Finally, in dispensationalist groups there are some psychological and social forces at work that make it difficult for dispensationalists to leave behind their accustomed patterns of biblical interpretation. To some extent cohesive social forces are at work in any culture or subculture with a shared world view and shared doctrines (see Berger and Luckmann). In itself this counts neither for nor against the truth of the world view or the doctrines. But it does mean that things that seem obvious or plain or commonsensical to members of a social group need not be at all obvious to those outside.

One special factor operative among dispensationalists is the reaction against the destructive forces associated with Darwinism. Darwinism together with the growth of other sciences has radically undermined the previous broad Western cultural commitment to a Christian or at least semi-Christian world view. Dispensationalism has answered the challenge of the supposed exact truths of the sciences with an exaltation of the exactitude of the truths of Scripture. Scriptural use of figurative, not-perfectly-clear, or not-perfectly-precise language can easily seem like a liability. Hence there is pressure on dispensationalists to believe that the Bible has a great degree of precision in its language and to interpret its language in the least figurative way possible. To leave dispensationalism might seem akin to leaving behind both the claims that the Bible can really stand up to the standards of modern science and the certainties obtained by operating with precise, everywhere-clear-cut language.

A second, related area of concern is the fear of subjectivity. Dispensationalists have seen modernists and cultists wrest the meaning of the Bible on the basis of subjective biases, biases often influenced by full-blown religious systems and world views. Dispensationalists naturally repudiate the use of these biases. An interpretation governed by subjectivity is deeply wrong, but fear of subjectivity easily leads to the rejection of explicit reflection on hermeneutics. Instead the Bible student simply appeals to the "plain" meaning of the text. The text hardly needs an interpreter's input since it stands there already with a "plain" meaning. To operate on this level gives the appearance of having the assurance of a maximum objectivity.

On the other hand, suppose we examine many hermeneutical principles *explicitly,* taking things less for granted. We may soon begin to realize that there are other possible options— options not only for the interpretation of this or that text, but for the formulation of hermeneutical principles. The principles themselves must be justified, partly by an appeal to texts. But then the process threatens to become circular, and we become much less confident about our objectivity.

Hermeneutical reflection can also include reflection on the influences of whole systems of interpretation. Theological systems, whether dispensationalist, covenantal, Calvinist, Arminian, or even modernist, have a profound influence on the way we approach a given text. World views and social context influence what we notice, what we assume as obvious, and what we emphasize.

THE NEAR IMPOSSIBILITY OF SIMPLE REFUTATIONS

Of course some dispensationalists have reflected and written about hermeneutics. But even these discussions sometimes assume principles that the nondispensationalist would like to make points of discussion and debate. In particular some dispensationalists still appear to the outsider to be working with a rather unanalyzed idea of the "plain meaning" of a text.

A third area of influence lies in the very fact that most dispensationalists are unaware of some social factors contributing to a unified dispensationalist reading of biblical texts. Dispensationalists have been at pains to insist that the Bible is plain and that therefore the interpreter should stick to the plain meaning. Unfortunately, because of the historical distance between us and biblical times, the original human authors' intentions are not always immediately plain to us. When we advise the average readers of the Bible that the meaning is "plain," what will they conclude? They will tend *not* to read it in its original historical context but in the context of the twentieth century, their own subcultural context. The Bible is thus regarded as a book written directly to modern people, not mainly to the original readers. Who, then, are the modern people whom the Bible addresses? Most immediately they are the circle of Christians within which a dispensationalist moves. To lay dispensationalists "plain" meaning is meaning that they automatically see in a text when they read it against the background of the teaching and examples that they have seen and heard from fellow Christians, most of whom are themselves dispensationalists. "Plain meaning" can all too easily become, in practice, the meaning of a text when seen through the framework of the dispensationalist system—or any system for that matter.

This immediately explains a number of frustrations that people experience in their encounters with another position. Too frequently nondispensationalists meet lay dispensationalists who are shocked to discover that anyone would hold views different from theirs. Their first reaction may be to wonder whether the nondispensationalist is a genuine Christian. This reaction is understandable if the hermeneutical stress on plainness has (1) discouraged dispensationalist pastors from alerting their congregations to differences of interpretation among Evangelicals, and (2) caused the members of the congregations to regard deviation from their in-group interpretation as a repudiation of the Bible itself (because the meaning is "plainly" there).

The same social tendency also explains the comparative infrequency, even among more scholarly classic dispensationalists, of extended reflection on the theological milieu of the first-century church. To nondispensationalist New Testament scholars, at least, most classic dispensationalist interpretation of the New Testament is all too obviously interpretation against the background of an already completed dispensationalist system, rather than a genuine attempt to read the books as written by first-century authors to first-century audiences. Since this no doubt does not seem to be the case to a dispensationalist, it is not a good debating point. But New Testament scholars often labor hard to "get inside" the writings of human authors of the Bible. They attempt to understand not only what the authors said but why they said it in the *way* that they did, trying to understand what sorts of concerns animated their lives and preaching.

Against the background of such concerns, a key question arises. Would the books of the New Testament have been written as they have in fact been written if their authors had been self-conscious classic dispensationalists? Nondispensationalist scholars do not think so.

Let us use an analogy. The New Testament teaching as a whole forms the basis on which the church subsequently worked out the creedal formulations of the Trinity and of the two natures of Christ. The creedal formulations are, I believe, firmly based on the New Testament and are in thorough harmony with biblical teaching. But the New Testament writers did not necessarily hold all these doctrines with the self-consciousness that was achieved in later synthesizing reflection. The apostles wrote the pure and final truth for our salvation. But it would be anachronistic to imagine that the apostles must necessarily have had the same self-conscious technical sophistication about Trinitarian questions as did Augustine or Gregory of Nazianzus. In saying this, we are not suggesting that Augustine was smarter than Paul, but merely that Augustine's conscious reflections focused in different directions from those of the apostle Paul. What all the apostles together taught in all the New Testament writings had implications that no one apostle may have ever had occasion to reflect on self-consciously.

Comparing this with the situation with respect to dispensationalism, I would claim that it is anachronistic to imagine that the apostles were self-conscious, sophisticated dispensationalists. Instead, a dispensationalist should simply claim to have correctly deduced and synthesized the later dispensationalist system from the totality of apostolic teachings, taken together. If this is so, historical understanding of the New Testament will take account of the apostles' distance in mentality from ourselves.

So we try to understand Matthew, Paul, John, and the author of Hebrews as much as possible on their own terms. To nondispensationalist scholars, at least, it seems that the New Testament authors just do not think like self-conscious classic dispensationalists. Nondispensationalists think that the New Testament authors were operating theologically in terms of a hermeneutics of fulfillment at odds with the basic principle of classic dispensationalism (on this hermeneutics, cf., e.g., Dodd, Longenecker). New Testament authors all may have been premillennialists, they all may have been amillennialists, or some may not have had a particular worked-out conviction. But all were oriented to the idea of fulfillment in Christ and then in his people, in both his first and his second comings. This central motif rather than the Millennium as such dominated teaching about the future.

Nevertheless in debating situations it is unadvisable to appeal to the first-century church. This is because many factors are involved in assessing the theological atmosphere of the first-century church and its bearing on understanding the New Testament.

The "sensationalistic" variety of dispensationalism (e.g., Hal Lindsey's *The Late Great Planet Earth*) can now also be better understood. Once the assumption is made that the Bible is written directly into one's own twentieth-century context, the attempt to make detailed correlations between the Bible and the latest political and social events is attractive. Granted the crucial assumption, the results are by no means ridiculous.

Finally, dispensationalists are concerned to preserve the purity of salvation by grace alone and to maintain the assurance grounded on this grace. The assurance of salvation is closely related to the faithfulness of God to his promises, but how are these promises construed? If they are not "plain," our assurance is threatened. Moreover, dispensationalists have been among those most zealous to defend the idea that many promises of God are unconditional, which guarantees their fulfillment in exactly the form that they are uttered. The desire for unconditionality may be one subtle factor behind the attractiveness of the ideal of scientifically precise language. In everyday language of the home or the workplace, a statement or a promise may include implicit qualifications or conditions. For instance, "I will be there at five o'clock" often may be said with the implicit understanding, "If no emergencies prevent me," or "If you do not cancel the engagement." On the other hand, in the scientific sphere we expect that qualifications or conditions will be spelled out. To assimilate the Bible to scientific language gives greater weight to the claim that there are many unconditional promises.

On this point variation exists. Most modified dispensationalists believe that the promises to Abraham concerning seed and land are unconditional but that our participation in the fulfillment is conditioned on faith. I can agree with this position.

EVALUATING SOCIAL FORCES

So much for social forces contributing to the stability and attractiveness of dispensationalism. We should notice that there is some element of *good* motivation and *good* principle behind each of these forces, but in each case what is good can undergo distortion.

Consider first the concern to have a reply to exact science. Behind the dispensationalist reaction is the good principle of the divine authority and trustworthiness of the Bible. But there is danger that in the zeal to maintain this principle, it may be distorted by the imposition of artificial modern standards of precision and technical language.

Next, what about the fear of subjectivity and the insistence on the plainness of the Bible? Here again a good principle is involved, namely the principle of the perspicuity of the Bible. The things necessary for salvation are said so clearly in one place or another that even the unlearned may come to a sufficient understanding of them. However, that does not mean that all parts of the Bible are equally clear; nor does it mean that even clear passages are clear in every respect. Hence it is not equivalent to the view that all or nearly all passages of the Bible have a meaning so evident that the average reader will immediately grasp it. The principle of perspicuity, like the principle of biblical inerrancy, is subject to oversimplification and distortion.

Next, what about the issue of the influence of tradition on interpretation? Over against the claims of the Roman Catholic church to exercise final control of the results of interpretation, the Reformers insisted that church tradition was not another authority alongside the Bible. Rather church tradition must continually be resubjected to the criticism of the Bible. Such subordination of tradition to the Bible is the element of truth in the dispensationalist tendency to eliminate any reckoning on church tradition. But again, the Reformation principle is not the same as saying that church tradition does not exist or that we can ever totally eliminate its influence on the way we interpret the Scriptures.

What about the dispensationalist love for salvation by grace and for unconditional promises? The element of truth in this dispensationalist concern is obvious and important. Christ fully accomplished our salvation and fully satisfied the justice of God by being our substitute. Hence salvation is guaranteed. It is unconditional in the sense that Christ fulfills all conditions. The Old Testament promises to Abraham rest ultimately on the grace to be given through the coming of Christ. But this guarantee will not eliminate the necessity of obedience and discipleship on the part of Christians. Christ's salvation and the assurance of salvation are only available to Christians in union with Christ, in the exercise of faith; and true faith is not dead faith, but faith that works by love (Gal. 5:6; cf. James 2). Precisely in the letter where Paul is contending so vigorously for pure grace (Gal. 5:4) and pure faith (3:2–14), he is not afraid to issue warnings to any who would have carnal assurance while they persevere in wickedness (Gal. 5:13–6:10, esp. 6:8). Paul boldly uses a statement with an "if," threatening eternal destruction on evildoers. A bare profession of faith (honor with the lips) not accompanied by a change in life and allegiance will not lead to eternal salvation: such faith is hypocritical. The unconditional language of other passages does not operate independently of this type of qualification. We must not oversimplify the New Testament teaching on grace and convert it into antinomianism. Hence it is simplistic to label every Old Testament statement about obedience and every statement mentioning a condition as merely law in antithetical opposition to grace. We are grateful that many leading contemporary dispensationalists do acknowledge this problem and are distancing themselves from the antinomian extreme of the past.

UNDERSTANDING DISPENSATIONALISTS

Notably, each of the social forces that we have discussed is related in some way to the desire for certainty. The most basic form of certainty concerns the basic truths of the Bible, including certainty of salvation. Bringing in the law with its stress of human responsibility and its threats might easily threaten the certainty of salvation. The sharp distinction between law and grace and the stress on unconditional promises therefore become attractive features of dispensationalism. We must remember that Darby himself inaugurated dispensationalism in the context of his own deliverance into the certainty of his heavenly standing in Christ.

Next, dispensationalism appeals to the desire for certainty concerning one's own role in a changing world. The progress of science seems to undermine one's confidence in the Bible, both because of the Darwinian view of man's origin and because of the assumption in much of science that the world is a big, self-governing mechanism. Over against this threat dispensationalism wants to confirm the reliability of the Bible. In the process, however, dispensationalism—especially with its emphasis on the literal—runs the danger of assimilating the Bible too much to the standards of modern science.

How do we evaluate the changes in the political and social worlds? Dispensationalism encourages a certain type of correlation between prophecy and our time. The establishment of correlation can provide adherents with a deep sense of orientation to and understanding of events that could otherwise easily be quite frightening and disquieting. By having the events integrated with the Bible as a reference point, the hearers are reassured concerning the correctness of their own position; and they are furnished with a stance to adopt. They have a coherent interpretation of the events. Sensationalistic dispensationalism can be very appealing for this reason.

Dispensationalism also offers certainty in *interpretation* to the ordinary Bible student. The subjectivities of non-Christian irrationalism and autonomy are very strong in our time. In contrast to these, dispensationalism asserts plainness. In apposition to the threat of sociological relativization, or the problems of doubt that can crop up in earnest theological debate, popular dispensationalism maintains a basic nonawareness of church tradition as an influencing factor in interpretation. Over against the scholarly difficulties and multitudes of unanswered questions involved in thoroughgoing grammatical-historical interpretation, dispensationalism assures its students of the availability of the Bible to the ordinary reader.

There is also of course the certainty involved in having a system. Any system (whether wholly correct or not) provides many answers, and to leave that system would seem almost like entering into a void. Therefore people would rather tolerate considerable difficulties or apparent contradictions in the system than leave because of them.

Not only dispensationalists, however, seek certainty in a system. Nondispensationalists also have a desire for certainty. And God does provide certainty and security in union with Jesus Christ. But we must ask ourselves, "Are we seeking another security than that of being one of Christ's sheep?" Being a sheep means being secure, not because one has all the answers, but because one is in Christ's care.

When we seek security in the wrong way, it affects our ability to help others. For instance, we may acquire the habit of blasting opponents just to justify ourselves and so reinforce our security in "being right." Or, conversely, we may retreat from any confrontation with the erring, for fear of being found deficient ourselves.

The analysis of dispensationalism up to this point is not really meant to show that dispensationalism is wrong. It is rather meant to give us all pause (dispensationalists and nondispensationalists alike). To the self-confident it says: There are influences on your beliefs that you do not fully realize. Bad motives or mixed motives, whether of yourself or of others, can damage the purity of your beliefs in subtle ways. Hidden assumptions that you have taken over uncritically from others may affect your understanding. Are you really certain that all your beliefs are from God? Is it possible that you might have accepted some of them because you respected the teachers who told you? Do not be so confident about details when you have not really considered an opponent's arguments in full.

Conversely, to the timid something must be said on the other side. You *must* use your gifts, including the educational benefits that you have received from your teachers, to spread in the church the knowledge that you have. You must teach and be bold about what the Bible has to say. But you do so subject to correction by others in the church. Listening to other Christians (including Christians outside your immediate circle of doctrine) is one of the ways God has given by which he guides us into truth.

6
STRATEGY FOR DIALOGUE WITH DISPENSATIONALISTS

What happens when people get into arguments for and against dispensationalism? While the first skirmishes are usually theological, with disagreements over doctrine, eschatological events, the relation of the Old Testament law to the Christian, or some other such question, the arguments soon involve particular verses of Scripture. People disagree over exegesis (the meaning one assigns to a particular passage); yet exegesis is not enough. The essence of the difference is over hermeneutics (general principles for interpreting the Bible). Dialogue will not get far unless it confronts the hermeneutical issues directly.

THE PERTINENCE OF EXEGESIS

Shall we then confine our arguments to the level of hermeneutical principle? No. Most dispensationalists are rightly suspicious of argument that appeals only to general principles, whether these principles are hermeneutical or theological. They want to see arguments based on particular texts. Hence observations with regard to hermeneutics are unlikely to be very useful or very effective unless they are tied in with exegesis (the interpretation of particular texts).

Exegesis, however, can easily become sidetracked by multiplying the number of texts under discussion. Well-trained dispensationalists and nondispensationalists alike have multitudes of texts at their disposal. When confronted with difficulties in the interpretation of one text, they appeal to another that they believe confirms their interpretation of the first text. The opponents quickly find themselves frustrated and often out of their depth because they not only cannot agree with the interpretation of even *one* of these texts, but they find themselves called on to reinterpret a large number of texts simultaneously. Since the texts can be discussed effectively and thoroughly only one at a time, the discussion may only confirm to each side the impression of its correctness and the obtuseness of the other side. Each side simply sees the text in the light of a gestalt, a system that itself is built up using many other texts. Those many other texts must be appealed to in order to explain the system thoroughly to the outsider.

As a nondispensationalist hoping to persuade dispensationalists, I have found two texts to be particularly useful in inviting classic dispensationalists to rethink some of their views: Hebrews 12:22–24 and, subordinately, 1 Corinthians 15:51–53. Classic dispensationalists are their own best judges of what passages they themselves would choose as a basis for discussion representing their side. Both kinds of discussion are helpful for the sake of learning from each other.

From here on, then, I will focus on Hebrews 12:22–24 and 1 Corinthians 15:51–53 and related hermeneutical questions, looking at ways that classic dispensationalists might be helped. Modified dispensationalists will also find these texts of interest in their dialogue with classic dispensationalists. Since modified dispensationalists and nondispensationalists display considerable variety among themselves, I am less certain which would be the best texts for a dialogue between them. Moreover, as we have seen (chapters 3 and 4), the views of the two groups approach each other closely at many points. Hebrews 12:22–24 and 1 Corinthians 15:51–53 will still be of considerable interest to them; but because of the greater measure of agreement, dialogue over these texts will take on a different complexion.

In the case of dialogue with classic dispensationalists, however, appeal to the texts in themselves is not enough. The texts need to be discussed in a way that appeals alternately to hermeneutical principles and to exegesis. Only in that way will the underlying hermeneutical principles come to the surface. By using the key texts, the interpreter can bring up the hermeneutical principles in a concrete way. This will help to show that hermeneutical practice in classic dispensationalism does not and cannot live up to its theory.

Aside from the above two texts, in general the best strategy for critics discussing particular texts is to admit freely that at least two interpretations of the text are possible: one that makes sense when one operates within a classic dispensationalist system, and one that makes sense when one operates within the critic's system. By operating this way critics can achieve two positive goals. First, they can build friendship with dispensationalist dialogue partners by showing that they are able to stand in the other person's shoes and listen sympathetically. They may learn more about the Bible, and they will learn more about what it is like to be a dispensationalist interpreter. They may say, "Yes, I see that by using these principles it makes sense to argue that the text means thus and so." This will help them not to make fun of things that seem unreasonable when viewed from *outside* the classic dispensationalist system. At the same time they can help make dispensationalists more aware of the way in which their system as a whole forms an all-important input for exegesis. Critics place over against one another two whole frameworks (a dispensationalist framework and their own nondispensationalist framework). Then they say, "Let us see how each system works when applied to a particular text." This approach makes it more apparent that the opponent's position is not simply a question of obtuseness over the meaning of one text, or lack of knowledge of the existence of some other supporting prooftext.

PARTICULAR THEOLOGICAL ISSUES

The theological issues separating dispensationalist Evangelicals from nondispensationalist Evangelicals are difficult to discuss briefly because they often involve the integration of the contents of a large number of biblical texts. Serious wrestling about theological integration is, in general, best left for times of reading and meditation on the Bible. But it is still helpful to set forth as succinctly as possible the theological issues so that dispensationalists can have the opportunity to reflect on them later. Three areas of reflection seem to me to be the most fruitful.

First, there is the issue of the church's inheritance of Old Testament promises.[1] The essence of the theological issue here

[1] I am indebted to Edmund P. Clowney for this argument.

can be posed very simply. To which Old Testament promises is Christ heir? Is he an Israelite? Is he the offspring of Abraham? Is he the heir of David? The answer must be, "No matter how many promises God has made, they are 'Yes' in Christ" (2 Cor. 1:20). Now to which of these promises are Christians heirs in union with Christ? Theologically it is hard to resist the answer "All of them." After all, "in Christ all the fullness of the Deity lives in bodily form, and you have been given fullness in Christ, who is the head over every power and authority" (Col. 2:9–10). One cannot neatly divide between heavenly and earthly blessings because there is only one Christ, and we receive the whole Christ. The resurrection of the body and the renewal of creation in Christ touch also the physical aspects of existence (Rom. 8:22–23). As Paul says, "He who did not spare his own Son, but gave him up for us all—how will he not also, along *with him,* graciously give us *all* things" (Rom. 8:32, emphasis mine). It is no exaggeration, then, when Paul says that the "world" (which must include the land of Palestine!) is ours (1 Cor. 3:21–23). We will return to this issue in chapters 12 and 13.

A second theological issue is that of the nature of Old Testament symbolism. The atmosphere of God's revelation in the Old Testament was an atmosphere suffused with eschatological hope. This hope focused on the last days and was oriented to God's heavenly dwelling. In that context the most literalistic reading of eschatological prophecy is not the best. We will take up this issue at greater length under the discussion of literalness (chapters 8–11).

Third, there is the issue of how the Bible itself is to be used in the controversy. Can we agree that one of the issues, perhaps the key issue, most distinguishing dispensationalists from nondispensationalists is the interpretation of the Old Testament? This issue includes within itself the question of dispensations or redemptive epochs, the question of Israel and the church, and the question of literalism in interpretation. Among all the types of Old Testament texts, Old Testament prophecy is the most in dispute. Hence, interpretation of prophecy is a key theological issue to consider.

How do we go about finding the Bible's own teaching on the interpretation of the Old Testament? By reading the Bible, of course. But that is a big project. Is there some particular passage of the Bible that addresses this issue more directly and speaks to it at great length? I believe there is: the whole Book of Hebrews. Thus we should carefully base our interpretation of the Old Testament *primarily* on this book. In the case of the doctrine of justification, for instance, we start with the two great passages of Romans 3–4 and Galatians 3. Then we integrate into the doctrine minor passages like James 2. What would happen if we reversed the procedure? Suppose we tried to fit the major passage or passages into a scheme that we had derived almost wholly from a few verses, verses whose implications might not be absolutely clear in themselves. We would be much more liable to error and distortion that way.

I propose, then, both to myself and to my dispensationalist friends, the following discipline. Let us all devote ourselves to reading, studying, and meditating on the Book of Hebrews. Let us ask the Lord to teach us how to interpret the Old Testament correctly, and how to properly understand the relation of the Old Testament to the New Testament. Let us not struggle to have Hebrews simply *confirm* our already existing views. Rather, let us cast those views aside so far as we genuinely can. Let us subject them to criticism wherever things in the Book of Hebrews point us in that direction. Let us be humble listeners, following wherever Hebrews leads us.

I do not think there is any danger in this discipline. The Bible is able to protect us from going astray. We do not need to cling tightly to our previous beliefs in order to be safe. In fact, we will not be safe if we are not open to having the Bible challenge even views that we dearly cherish.

Moreover, I think that something like this procedure is probably the ideal way for people who are unsure of their own position to make up their minds. No doubt one of the reasons God has provided us with the Book of Hebrews is so that we would have a safe and sure starting point and guide into the complexities of interpreting the Old Testament. It has proved to be that in my life: the above discipline helped me to make up my mind. I sincerely believe that it will be equally effective in many other lives, too.

The extensive size of the Book of Hebrews (thirteen chapters) precludes giving a full discussion of it here. Chapter 12 of this book, however, focuses attention on a key passage of Hebrews, namely 12:22–24.

7
THE LAST TRUMPET

Before discussing the crucial question of the principle of literal interpretation, it is well for us to look at a particular example that illustrates several of the problems. First Corinthians 15:51–53 brings us into confrontation with some of the hermeneutical principles that bear directly on our discussion. Although this passage is by no means decisive in a discussion of dispensationalism, it is an effective preliminary step in establishing positive relationships of communication.

FIRST CORINTHIANS 15:51–53 AS A PROBLEM TO PRETRIBULATIONALISM

Because it speaks of "the *last* trumpet," 1 Corinthians 15:51–53 presents a problem to classic dispensationalist doctrine, which interprets the passage as referring to a pretribulational rapture. Seven years *after* the Rapture, *another* trumpet is sounded at the visible second coming of Christ, in connection with the gathering of the elect Jews (Matt. 24:31). Hence the trumpet sound described in 1 Corinthians 15:52 apparently is not the *last* trumpet. If, on the other hand, the rapture of 1 Corinthians 15:51–53 and the visible second coming of Matthew 24:31 are essentially simultaneous (contrary to classic dispensationalist theory), the two trumpets are presumably also the same, and there is no difficulty.

There is thus an obvious problem in reconciling 1 Corinthians 15:51–53 and Matthew 24:31 with dispensationalist theory. The standard dispensationalist answer to this difficulty is fairly obvious within their system. Those familiar enough with the general principles of dispensationalism may be able to figure it out for themselves. My concern, however, is not with whether there is an answer, but with the hermeneutical question of how the answer is obtained.

One must in effect keep raising hermeneutical questions. What are the *principles* we use to understand 1 Corinthians 15:51–53 and to reconcile it with Matthew 24:31? When classic dispensationalists talk about those principles, they tell us that we must interpret "literally" or "plainly"; so what is a literal interpretation of 1 Corinthians 15:51–53? To be literal could mean simply to take fully into account all the grammatical, contextual, and historical clues throwing light on this passage. Such a procedure is sometimes demanding. But it would be sound. On the other hand, to be literal could imply that we are to stick to what is most plain or obvious. If we agreed with this principle, we would argue as follows:

> The "plain" meaning of 1 Corinthians 15:52 seems to be that this is the *last* trumpet. Therefore there cannot be any more trumpets after that one. You have told us to be literal; we cannot make it out as saying anything else if we are "literal." Now when we turn to Matthew 24:31, and it speaks of a trumpet, we are bound to believe that Matthew's trumpet is either the same one or an earlier one. After all the one in 1 Corinthians 15:52 is the "last" trumpet (*literally* the last). Matthew 24:30 already speaks of the visible Second Coming. Hence it appears that the visible Second Coming is simultaneous with the transformation of believers' bodies in the Rapture. Because you have told us to be literal in interpreting 1 Corinthians 15:51–53, we cannot believe in the seven-year distinction between the Rapture and the Second Coming.

There might be several suggestions for avoiding this conclusion. First, one could suggest that though there is only one trumpet, there are several blasts from the trumpet. But this suggestion will not work, because 1 Corinthians 15:52 mentions the trumpet *sound*. It clearly implies that this is the last *sounding* of a trumpet of God, not merely that there is a single fixed trumpet that is used for blasts relating to a long series of last events.

Next one could suggest that the trumpet sound is perhaps

seven years long. But this suggestion will not work because of the stress in 1 Corinthians 15:52 on the quickness of the operation. The raising of the dead sequentially follows the sounding of the trumpet, rather than taking place during some very long sounding of the trumpet. Or at least this seems to be the "plainest" way to take the text.

Or one could suggest that Matthew 24:31 is not about the visible second coming of Christ but about the Rapture. But a literal interpretation of Matthew 24:30 would certainly lead us to think that we are dealing with the visible Second Coming.

The above argument arose from trying to be literal in a wooden sense. But even if we are trying just to understand 1 Corinthians 15 and Matthew 24 by sound, grammatical-historical exegesis, these texts are most easily reconciled by viewing the Rapture and the Second Coming as simultaneous.

THE STANDARD DISPENSATIONALIST ANSWER

J. Dwight Pentecost (pp. 189–91) sets forth the standard dispensationalist answer to the dilemma of the trumpet:

> The word *last* may signify that which concludes a program, but is not necessarily the last that will ever exist. Inasmuch as the program for the church differs from that for Israel, each may be terminated by the blowing of a trumpet, properly called the last trumpet, without making the two last trumpets identical and synonymous [*sic;* a later edition corrects this to "synchronous"] as to time.
>
> . . . (3) The trumpet for the church is singular. No trumpets have preceded it so that it can not be said to be the last of a series. The trumpet that closes the tribulation period is clearly the last of a series of seven. . . . (7) The trumpet in 1 Thessalonians is distinctly for the church. Since God is dealing with Israel in particular, and the Gentiles in general, in the tribulation, this seventh trumpet, which falls in the period of the tribulation, could not have reference to the church without losing the distinctions between the church and Israel.

Pentecost has more to say, though much of it is only relevant against the theory of midtribulationist rapture or in the context of particular, specialized views concerning the seventh trumpet in Revelation 11:15.

Pentecost is certainly right on one point: in some contexts "last" should not be understood in an absolute sense. But how do we decide when the word "last" is to be understood in a qualified way? What hermeneutical principle do we use? What does it mean to interpret "last" literally? Sometimes "last" is accompanied by a qualifying genitive: "On the last and greatest day *of the Feast*" (John 7:37, emphasis mine). "Last" may receive a qualification obvious from the context: "last" in Matthew 20:8 must mean last of those hired. But 1 Corinthians 15:51–53 has no such obvious qualification. On the contrary, the passage as a whole is about events that the first-century Jewish environment associated with the end of the whole world. The perspective is cosmic, not some limited series of events.

In the end Pentecost really has only one hermeneutical argument for not understanding "last" in an unqualified way: it is last for the *church,* not for Israel. But where does 1 Corinthians say or hint that the "lastness" is to be understood as confined to the concerns of the church? Dispensationalists agree that the scope of 1 Corinthians 15:20–28 includes the whole millennial period, up to the consummation. And 15:45–57 is obviously picking up many of the topics of 15:20–28. Dispensationalists have told us to be literal. Literal interpretation no doubt must include not reading things into the text that have no warrant for being there.

As dispensationalists wrestle with the explanation and interpretation of 1 Corinthians 15:52, the question needs to be asked repeatedly, "What does 'literal' interpretation of 1 Corinthians 15:51–53 mean?" Ultimately for Pentecost "literalness" appears to mean reading 1 Corinthians 15:51–53 with the Israel/church distinction already in mind. It means coming to the passage and asking whether it is speaking of Israel's destiny or the church's. But that would mean that the word "literal" is so loaded with the connotations of dispensationalism that it is worthless for the purpose of positive and fair dialogue.

All interpreters with a high view of the Bible's doctrinal unity agree that we are to strive to understand one passage of the Bible in a way that harmonizes with other passages. Any one passage should be read not only in terms of its immediate literary and historical context, but in terms of the context of the whole Bible. Interpreters, however, will have already formed a host of doctrinal convictions about the overall teaching of the Bible. They will be reluctant to abandon the convictions that they have developed on the basis of the clear teaching of several texts just because one new text appears to present difficulties. Hence what dispensationalists are doing with 1 Corinthians 15:51–53 is not so very different from what nondispensationalists do; both read texts under the influence of prior judgments and convictions. It must be recognized, however, that this process makes it more difficult for people to abandon error.

By itself, then, this brief analysis of 1 Corinthians 15:51–53 does not show that dispensationalists are wrong. It is useful, nevertheless, to increase our awareness of the way in which the dispensationalist system impinges on the interpretation of a given passage. The system does affect interpretation. This analysis is useful also because similar effects occur at various points within any system of interpretation. No one escapes all the problems.

The problems are more acute, however, within classic dispensationalism, which maintains a sharp two-peoples-of-God distinction. Classic dispensationalism, whether right or wrong, is almost impossible to refute by an appeal to texts. The aid of the dispensationalist system almost automatically provides a way out of otherwise problematic texts. The word "literal" can conceal these differences because it is not clear how much that word allows. Does "literalism" permit the importation of the distinction between Israel and the church at any point where the system gets into difficulty? If so, "literalism" begs the most important interpretive questions that are at stake with nondispensationalists.

What do dispensationalists themselves say about how a system can be refuted? Charles Feinberg's description (p. 39) of testing premillennialism goes as follows:

> First, when certain difficulties are affirmed of a doctrine which claims to be biblical, one is only required to show that a solution of the alleged problem is possible. When certain passages are referred to that are said to contradict the premillennial doctrine, all that is necessary is to demonstrate that according to the rules of exegesis, a harmonization is possible.

To begin with, postmillennialism and amillennialism as well as modified dispensationalism and nondispensationalist versions of premillennialism could each hold its own on the same basis as Feinberg suggests. Each one has to demonstrate that "harmonization is possible" within its own system. Surely all firm premillennialists, postmillennialists, and amillennialists claim that much. Feinberg's criteria are really too weak to arbitrate between different millennial positions.

But the problem is worse yet, because Feinberg is still vague about what "the rules of exegesis" are. Do these rules include the right to invoke the Israel/church distinction when dealing with a passage like 1 Corinthians 15:51–53? If they do, we are involved in a circular argument. The circle goes as follows. Premillennial dispensationalism demonstrates the validity of an Israel/church distinction. This distinction is incorporated into a hermeneutical rule. And that rule is used to build up and harmonize the dispensational system.

Feinberg's continuation (p. 40) is not reassuring:

> Every prophecy is part of a wonderful scheme of revelation; for the true significance of any prophecy, the whole prophetic scheme must be kept in mind and the interrelationship between the parts in the plan as well.

Feinberg seems to be saying that the entire dispensationalist system ought to be kept in mind as one is interpreting any one prophecy. It sounds as if the essentials of dispensationalism have been incorporated into the rules of exegesis. Perhaps not. Perhaps Feinberg is working with a distinction between exegesis in a narrow sense (the first quotation above) and the application of the "significance" of a prophecy in a broad sense (the second quotation above). But exegesis in a narrow sense would certainly not do with 1 Corinthians 15:51–53 what dispensationalists do with it.

We are left, then, with a big problem. What is literal interpretation, and what will we allow to be taken into account in the interpretation of any one text? Moreover, how do we avoid an unfruitful circularity in dialogue? Feinberg is not the only one who could fall into circularity. One can imagine the classic dispensationalist, the modified dispensationalist, the amillennialist, and the postmillennialist alike going round and round, showing that it is possible to harmonize texts with their respective systems. Each system will establish its case all the more effectively if, as is often the case, the "rules of exegesis" are understood with a slightly different slant within the various systems. The appeal to literalism is often seen as part of the avoidance of subjectivity in interpretation, but one does not really escape the possibility of subjectivity by simply waving "literalism" as a banner. It is necessary to examine what one means by that word and to try to specify what it does and does not imply. Otherwise one only hides from intellectual challenges and from insight into one's assumptions and limitations.

I am not saying that all dispensationalists are hiding, but those who are not might well take into account that others are.

8
WHAT IS LITERAL
INTERPRETATION?

In a sense nearly all the problems associated with the dispensationalist-nondispensationalist conflict are buried beneath the question of literal interpretation. We might already suspect as much after having reviewed Darby's and Scofield's approach to literalness. Their approaches toward strict literalness seem to be subordinated to the more fundamental principle of dual destinations for Israel and the church. For example, Scofield freely encourages the use of nonliteral, even "allegorical," meanings of Old Testament history. "Absolute literalness" is found in prophecy, and this literalness is quite compatible with the existence of many "figures" in prophetic speech (Scofield, *Scofield Bible Correspondence School,* pp. 45–46). So what Scofield means by "literal" is not too clear. Perhaps the word has already unconsciously been loaded with some of the assumptions belonging to the theological system.

Not all dispensationalist interpreters use the word "literal" in the same way. Modified dispensationalists, for instance, may use the word simply to refer to grammatical-historical interpretation. With them it has no other special meaning. In that case I do not disagree with them. But in much of the published dispensational literature there are added connotations. Hence we must examine this key word more closely.

DIFFICULTIES WITH THE MEANING OF "LITERAL"

To define literal interpretation is not so easy as it might appear. Ryrie (*Dispensationalism Today,* pp. 86–87) invokes other, related terms like "normal" and "plain" to explicate what he means by literalness. But by itself this explanation is not enough. Our sense of normality depends radically on our sense of context, including a whole world view, as Fish shows ("Normal Circumstances," pp. 625–44). Without repeating the contents of Fish's article, let me proceed to examine the problem by a parallel route.

One major aspect of the problem of defining "literal" is that in many instances words, but not sentences, have a literal or normal meaning. Moreover, for both words and sentences context is all-important in determining meaning at any given point in an act of communication. What contexts are to be looked at, and how they are to be looked at, in the determination of meaning is very important. Because questions of context are too often begged in classic dispensationalist discussion of literalness, we need to deal with these questions more precisely.

THE MEANING OF WORDS

We may best approach the central issue using some examples. Let us start with the following sample from a piece of writing:

battle

What does the word mean? We recognize that the graphic symbol "battle" can be either a noun ("a battle") or a verb ("to battle"). When we are not given any further context, we would most likely construe this as a noun. The verb, in fact, derives its meaning from the noun, rather than vice versa. If a large number of people were stopped on the street and asked to define "battle," the vast majority would probably give a definition like "a part of a war, a fight" (noun), rather than "to engage in combat" (verb). They would thereby indicate that they were thinking of the noun form rather than the verb.

This example shows that for most words there is something like a first-thought meaning, a meaning that one would naturally give when asked, "What does this word mean?" Not everyone might say exactly the same thing, but one aspect of the word would usually dominate.

When, however, we are given even a little bit of context, our guesses about the meaning may change radically. Let us see:

to battle

Now we are almost certain that "battle" is a verb. (But "to battle" could be a prepositional phrase, as in "Off to battle we go.") There is still a kind of "first-thought" meaning, namely, "to engage in combat, to fight." Let us have a little more context:

I had thorns and briers to battle

Now we are in difficulty. What is the literal meaning of this clause? If we insist that each word keep its first-thought meaning, we are unable to come up with a consistent interpretation. There is a tension between the verb "battle," which suggests an animate opponent, and the "thorns and briers," which are indicated as the opponent but are not animate. The statement is presumably metaphorical. But of course there is still an interpretation that results in (roughly) a minimum amount of figurativeness. For instance, a gardener might use such a statement as a colorful way to express problems in gardening. The word "battle" would have a figurative sense equivalent to "keep out." But of course the metaphorical statement hints at a little more than a minimum meaning. It invites us to toy with a whole set of analogies between military and agricultural affairs. Are there agricultural equivalents to weapons? Are there stages in the agricultural "battle" when it may appear that one side is "defeated," only to have the fortunes reversed? The use of "battle" suggests a little more than would the use of "keep out." We can judge *how* much more only when we see the context and know whether it exploits further comparisons between war and agriculture.

Would that I had thorns and briers to battle.

Having "would that" attached to the front of the sentence results in a global change in our estimate of the meaning. Whereas before we guessed that we had to do with an *actual* experience of a gardener, now we know that the experience is only a hypothetical, imagined one.

Let us see still more context:

Would that I had thorns and briers to battle! I would
    set out against them, I would burn them up
    together.

With this much context we can see that more extended analogies are developing between warfare and agriculture. "Set out against them" and "burn them up" are actions that one could do in warfare against cities. But a minimally figurative interpretation might maintain that all this analogy of warfare is brought in to illuminate the farmer's skills against thorns and briers.

> "A pleasant vineyard, sing of it!
>   I, the LORD, am its keeper;
>   every moment I water it.
> Lest any one harm it,
>   I guard it night and day;
>   I have no wrath.
> Would that I had thorns and briers to battle!
>   I would set out against them,
>   I would burn them up together.

This quotation sounds like a picture of the Garden of Eden, either Eden of the past or a new Eden of the future. We tend to suspect an allusion to Eden all the more because the mention of the Lord suggests the context of biblical revelation. In that context the Genesis story involving the Garden of Eden is an obvious backdrop. We therefore suspect that Eden is being alluded to. Yet no explicit statement makes it absolutely necessary to think of Eden. If we were quite wooden and unimaginative, we could say, "This passage is *just* saying that the Lord has a vineyard that he is committed to caring for. It is not saying that the vineyard is a new Eden or an old Eden."

Actually this passage comes from Isaiah 27:1–4 (RSV). When I say that much, I give people the opportunity to take into account much larger contexts: the context of Isaiah 27, of the whole Book of Isaiah, of Isaiah the person and his times, and of the portions of the Bible that were written before and after Isaiah. In particular, Isaiah 27:6 says that "Israel shall blossom and put forth shoots." In the light of that statement and the vineyard analogy in Isaiah 5, everyone will agree that Isaiah 27:2–4 is in fact using the entire picture of gardener and vineyard metaphorically. The "battling" of Isaiah 27:4 designates hypothetical battles that the Lord might fight against personal enemies. Though the whole picture is metaphorical, the particular word "battle" turns out to be used less metaphorically than we thought at first. Battles against personal enemies (more or less literal battles) are in view. Moreover, the effect of the word "battle" depends on our retaining a sense of the atmosphere of warfare as well as the way in which a gardener's struggles with thorns and briers are analogous to war.

In addition, it seems to me that when we take into account the total context the allusion to Eden is indeed present. The model of peace in Eden is used to evoke the comprehensive peace that Israel will experience in the future. This peace doubtless manifests itself primarily in a spiritual and social way, but the fruitfulness in view still seems to suggest the inclusion of literal agricultural bounty. It thus links up with the Deuteronomic blessings (Deut. 28:1–14) and prophetic predictions involving plant life (e.g., Isa. 32:15–20; 35:1–2).

We should notice, however, that a good many of these ideas are suggested or hinted at rather than said in so many words. We could not prove that the allusions were there to people who insisted on rock-solid evidence before they abandoned the most prosaic and limited interpretation.

DEFINING LITERALNESS

In the light of the foregoing example, we can say that there are at least three plausible ways of talking about literal meaning.

First, one could say that the literal meaning of a word is the meaning that native speakers are most likely to think of when they are asked about the word in isolation (that is, apart from any context in a particular sentence or discourse). This I have above called "first-thought" meaning. Thus the first-thought meaning of "battle" is "a fight, a combat." The first-thought meaning is often the most common meaning; it is sometimes, but not always, more "physical" or "concrete" in character than other possible dictionary meanings, some of which might be labeled "figurative." For example the first-thought meaning of "burn" is "to consume in fire." It is more "physical" and "concrete" than the metaphorical use of "burn" for burning anger. The first-thought meaning, or literal meaning in this sense, is opposite to any and all figurative meanings.

We have said that the first-thought meaning is the meaning for words in isolation. But what if the words form a sentence? We can imagine proceeding to interpret a whole sentence or a whole paragraph by mechanically assigning to each word its first-thought meaning. This would often be artificial or even

WHAT IS LITERAL INTERPRETATION?

absurd. It would be an interpretation that did not take into account the influence of context on the determination of which sense or senses of a word are actually activated. We might call such an interpretation "first-thought interpretation." As an example consider again the text "Would that I had thorns and briers to battle!" What would first-thought interpretation of this passage be like? First-thought meaning of "thorns" (the word in isolation) is "plant with prickly spines." First-thought meaning of "briers" is similar. First-thought meaning of "battle" is "military action against an opposing army." Adding these together in a purely mechanical way, we might obtain the result that the speaker wished to use briers and thorns as weapons in the next military campaign, or that thorns and briers had suddenly been transformed into a science fiction scenario where they actually organize themselves (consciously) into an army. Clearly first-thought interpretation is sometimes strange or absurd.

Next, we could imagine reading passages as organic wholes, but reading them in the most prosaic way possible. We would allow ourselves to recognize obvious figures of speech, but nothing beyond the most obvious. We would ignore the possibility of poetic overtones, irony, wordplay, or the possibly figurative or allusive character of whole sections of material. At least we would ignore such things whenever they were not perfectly obvious. Let us call this "flat interpretation." It is literal *if possible*.

Again let us take Isaiah 27:2–4 as our example. Flat interpretation recognizes that this passage is embedded in the rest of Isaiah 27 and Isaiah 27 in turn is embedded in the whole Book of Isaiah. But Isaiah 27:2–5 is taken simply as a prediction that the Lord will construct a perfect horticultural work in the form of a vineyard. Admittedly Isaiah 27:6—"Israel shall blossom"—is figurative for the spiritual prosperity of the *people* of Israel. So it is natural to take Isaiah 27:2–5 as an allusion to spiritual prosperity. But there is nothing to *prove* this conclusion. Isaiah 27:2–5 may be purely about agriculture. It is then related to Isaiah 27:6 only in terms of the common general theme of prosperity. Moreover, the purely agricultural reading is the most "literal." It is as close as possible to first-thought interpretation without falling into absurdity. Hence, since it is possible, it is the flat interpretation.

If this seems too extreme, we could take a more moderate

case. Suppose a person admits that Isaiah 27:2–5 is a figurative description of God's spiritual favor to Israel. Yet the person might still claim that there is no allusion to the Garden of Eden. No one could prove this wrong beyond any possibility of dispute, since Eden is not explicitly mentioned in the passage. This too is flat interpretation. But it is not as flat as the interpretation of the previous paragraph. I think it is convenient to retain the term "flat interpretation" as a designation of the most extreme case and then recognize that there may be other interpretations that would approach this extreme by degrees.

Finally, we may speak of a third kind of interpretation. In this type one reads passages as organic wholes and tries to understand what each passage expresses against the background of the original human author and the original situation. One asks what understanding and inferences would be justified or warranted at the time the passage was written. This interpretation aims to express the meanings that human authors express. Also it is willing to recognize fine-grained allusions and open-ended language. It endeavors to recognize when authors leave a degree of ambiguity and vagueness about how far their allusions extend. Let us call this "grammatical-historical interpretation."

If the author is a very unimaginative or prosaic sort of person, or if the passage is part of a genre of writing that is thoroughly prosaic, the grammatical-historical interpretation of the passage coincides with the flat interpretation. But in other cases flat interpretation and grammatical-historical interpretation will *not* always coincide. If the author is trying to be more imaginative, then it is an allowable part of grammatical-historical interpretation for us to search for allusions, wordplays, and other indirect ways of communicating, even when such things are not so obvious that no one misses them.

Now what do dispensationalist interpreters mean by "literal"? Do they mean one of the above types of interpretation or something different from any of them? Dispensationalists have said repeatedly that they recognize that there are figures of speech in the Bible. On the basis of that affirmation, and on the basis of the clearest and best of their statements on interpretive principles, we should presumably understand them to be advocating grammatical-historical interpretation. Moreover, in the history of hermeneutical theory, the term *sensus literalis* ("literal sense") has been associated with grammatical-historical interpretation. Therefore there is some historical warrant for using the word "literal" in a technical sense, simply to designate the aim of grammatical-historical interpretation. Nevertheless in our modern context the repeated use of the word "literal" by dispensationalists is not helpful. "Literal" tends to be understood as the opposite of "figurative." Thus the word "literal" may quite easily suggest the two other types of interpretation above (first-thought interpretation or flat interpretation).

"PLAIN" INTERPRETATION

The word "plain," which has been used as an alternative to "literal," is not much better. The original listeners to a piece of communication already have tacit awareness of a full-blown context: they are aware of the context of their historical situation, the context of their knowledge of grammar, and the context of the part of the communication that they have already heard. Because they have thoroughly absorbed these rich contexts *before* they hear the next sentence, that sentence will (ordinarily) seem to them to have a plain meaning. But if we as twentieth-century hearers read the same sentence and ask ourselves what its plain meaning is, what we will get is the meaning that the sentence or paragraph would have if occurring in our twentieth-century context—the context that is an inextricable part of *our* tacit knowledge. Sometimes the grammatical-historical meaning is not at all "plain" to us because we must work hard to try to reconstruct and appreciate the differences between then and now. Moreover, for lay dispensationalists the plain meaning will be the meaning that occurs to them in the context of their already existing knowledge of the prophetic system of dispensationalism.

This leads us to the possibility of still a fourth type of interpretation. "Plain interpretation," let us say, is interpretation of a text by interpreters against the context of the interpreters' tacit knowledge of their *own* world view and historical situation. It minimizes the role of the original historical and cultural context. Grammatical-historical interpretation differs from plain interpretation precisely over the question of the primary historical and cultural context for interpretation. Plain interpretation reads everything as if it were written directly to oneself, in one's own time and culture. Grammatical-historical interpretation reads everything as if it were written in the time and culture of the original author. Of course when we happen to be interpreting modern literature written in our own culture or subculture, the two are the same.

We have now seen that there are certain liabilities to the words "literal" and "plain." If dispensationalists are dead serious about advocating grammatical-historical interpretation, in distinction from first-thought interpretation, flat interpretation, and plain interpretation, I think they could demonstrate their commitment by dropping the phrase "literal interpretation." "Grammatical-historical interpretation" unambiguously designates what they want, whereas the word "literal" is ambiguous and tends wrongly to suggest some or all of the alternatives to grammatical-historical interpretation.

Of course the word "literal" could still be used to describe individual words that are being used in a nonfigurative sense. For instance the word "vineyard" literally means a field growing grapes. In Isaiah 27:2 it is used nonliterally, figuratively, as a designation for Israel. By contrast, in Genesis 9:20 the word is used literally (nonfiguratively). In these instances the word "literal" is the opposite of "figurative." But since any extended passage might or might not contain figures of speech, the word "literal" would no longer be used to describe a global method or approach to interpretation.

I suspect, however, that dropping the phrase "literal interpretation" might prove difficult for some dispensationalists, because "literal" has become a watchword or banner. It is a useful watchword, I suggest, precisely because it can become a vehicle for sliding into a flat interpretation or plain interpretation when it is convenient to do so.

9
DISPENSATIONALIST
EXPOSITIONS OF LITERALNESS

We now consider some of the more precise statements about literal interpretation that are made by dispensationalists. In particular, we want to see whether they avoid the difficulties that we have discussed.

RYRIE'S DESCRIPTION OF LITERALNESS

One of the fuller discussions of literal interpretation is set forth by Ryrie in *Dispensationalism Today* (pp. 86–87). The most important paragraph in his discussion is a long one; so for convenience we will analyze it a few sentences at a time. After some introductory remarks, Ryrie begins as follows:

> Dispensationalists claim that their principle of hermeneutics is that of literal interpretation. This means interpretation which gives to every word the same meaning it would have in normal usage, whether employed in writing, speaking or thinking.

Ryrie undoubtedly sees himself as heading toward a definition of grammatical-historical interpretation. Yet the above two sentences by themselves might very easily be construed as advocating first-thought interpretation in the sense defined on pages 82–85. That is, it might be construed as saying that each word is to be given the most prominent meaning that it has in the dictionary (first-thought meaning), regardless of context. Ryrie needs a much more complicated and qualified statement if he is to describe the decisive influence of historical context, discourse context, and sentence context on the question of *which* senses of a word (often, out of a whole range of senses found in a dictionary) are activated in a single given context.

Let us not, however, be too hard on Ryrie until we hear the continuation.

> This is sometimes called the principle of grammatical-historical interpretation since the meaning of each word is determined by grammatical and historical considerations.

This statement seems to be a good qualification. Yet Ryrie is still focusing on the meaning of *words*. Such a focus is not enough. His statements might still be presupposing an inadequate view of how *sentence* meaning and *discourse* meaning arise. The meaning of a sentence is not simply a mechanical sum of the meanings of its constituent words. There is grammar and paragraph context and historical context telling the reader how the words fit together, how they mutually qualify and modify one another in a complex interaction resulting in a communication of statements, commands, speaker attitudes, tone, allusions, and so on.

Ryrie continues:

> The principle might also be called normal interpretation since the literal meaning of words is the normal approach to their understanding in all languages.

Here Ryrie unfortunately gives the appearance of talking about first-thought interpretation. Is he saying that we should assign to each word in a passage the "literal" meaning, that is, the meaning that would first be thought of when the word is produced in isolation? At the very least Ryrie has still not moved beyond words into sentences and communicative acts. In charity we must suppose that, despite the apparent tendency of this sentence, Ryrie is *not* really advocating first-thought interpretation. Perhaps he wanted to say something like the following:

> Words appearing in a dictionary often have several possible meanings and have a potential to be used metaphorically. However when a given word appears in a certain passage, in a certain total context, one almost automatically assigns to it a meaning agreeing with the context. This almost automatic assignment (from the standpoint of a native

speaker) is what I mean by "literal meaning." Since this is also the normal way of proceeding, it can be called one aspect of normal interpretation.

Unfortunately Ryrie has not gone to any great care in defining some special sense for his phrase "the literal meaning of words." Hence it sounds as if what he means is first-thought meaning.
Let us look at the next sentence to see whether we get clarification.

It might also be designated plain interpretation so that no one receives the mistaken notion that the literal principle rules out figures of speech.

The mention of figures of speech is a useful qualification. Now the question will be whether, without "ruling out" figures of speech, Ryrie is nevertheless setting up a bias for flat interpretation (not to mention plain interpretation in my sense). Flat interpretation recognizes obvious figures of speech, but nothing beyond the obvious. The word "plain" might easily connote a refusal to go beyond the most obvious level. In that case it would be similar to plain interpretation as set forth on pages 85–86. Ryrie would be saying that (possibly because the differences between our times and biblical times are rather minimal) it is sufficient for us to interpret the Bible against the background of our own knowledge and culture. In view of what Ryrie said previously about "grammatical-historical consideration," I think that he does not want to talk about plain interpretation in my sense of the term (p. 85). In that case it would have been better if Ryrie had introduced more qualification or explanation.
Let us go on still further, to see whether Ryrie says anything to eliminate the option of flat interpretation or to reinforce that option.

Symbols, figures of speech and types are all interpreted plainly in this method and they are in no way contrary to literal interpretation. After all, the very existence of any meaning for a figure of speech depends on the reality of the literal meaning of the terms involved. Figures often make the meaning plainer, but it is the literal, normal, or plain meaning that they convey to the reader.

Does this explanation help? Well for me at least it does not. I cannot say that I know from this whether Ryrie is talking about what I call grammatical-historical interpretation or what I call flat interpretation. The word "literal" occurs here in three successive sentences. In the first we might hope that it is equivalent in meaning to "grammatical-historical." In the second sentence it means first-thought meaning (literal as the opposite of figurative). In the third it might very well suggest flat interpretation. This seems to me to confirm my impression that part of the value of the word "literal" is that it can slide between several different senses.

Moreover, the above description does not help us become aware of the possibilities involved with open-ended texts. Some texts may make clear their central aspects of meaning, but there may be mysteries about just how far certain allusions or suggested meanings are to be considered. Flat interpretation fails precisely here. It underestimates the possibilities for ambiguities and possible-but-not-perfectly-obvious allusions used for positive effects.

There is still a possible rejoinder to this problem. The proponents of flat interpretation might argue as follows:

> We grant that authors may produce open-ended texts. And we grant that it is improper to interpret such texts "flatly." But we think that the Bible is *not* an open-ended text. God, in writing the Bible, intended to communicate truth rather than conceal it. Hence we expect that he will *not* use ambiguity or not-so-clear allusion. He will *not* exploit poetic possibilities in open-ended metaphors (where we are not sure how far a metaphorical comparison extends).

This is a responsible position, but it is a position that needs to be argued for rather than simply assumed. It is easy to assume it without argument if we are not careful in stating hermeneutical principles. Moreover, I for one simply do not think that the position is true. Jesus' parables (see Mark 4:11–13) and types in the Old Testament appear to me to be the simplest counterexamples.

Ryrie, of course, mentions types explicitly in the material that I quoted. But what does he intend to do with them? In particular, does he think that the significance of an Old Testament type may go beyond what can be seen in the original Old Testament context? Some, perhaps most, interpreters with an orthodox view of biblical inspiration would say yes. The argument would be as follows. God knows the end from the beginning. Therefore, as the divine author of the Bible, he can establish a relation between the type and its antitypical fulfillment. Since the fulfillment comes only later, the type becomes richer than what is available by ordinary means in Old Testament times. In other words the divine intention for a type may, in certain cases, be richer than what one can obtain by grammatical-historical interpretation. Such richness, properly conceived, will not *violate* grammatical-historical meaning, or go contrary to it. The richness will arise from the added significance to the type when it is compared to the fulfillment.

If our observation about types is true, then grammatical-historical interpretation is not all that there is to the interpretation of types. Grammatical-historical interpretation is only one moment in the total act of interpretation. Hence it may be that Ryrie is not talking only about grammatical-historical interpretation. By mentioning types he may be thinking of principles that are richer than grammatical-historical interpretation. On the other hand, by not clearly excluding flat interpretation, he may be introducing a bias in favor of something less rich than grammatical-historical interpretation (because it will not take into account the allusions and figures that are not obvious). All in all there is still considerable leeway in Ryrie's delineation of what he means by literal interpretation.

Ryrie, using a quote from E. R. Craven, continues:

> The *literalist* (so called) is not one who denies that *figurative* language, that *symbols,* are used in prophecy, nor does he deny that great *spiritual* truths are set forth therein; his position is, simply, that the prophecies are to be *normally* interpreted (i.e., according to the received laws of language) as any other utterances are interpreted—that which is manifestly figurative being so regarded.

This quote is basically good. But Ryrie (or Craven, who is quoted) unfortunately does not tell us what to do when something is not "manifestly figurative." That is, suppose something is not obviously, plainly, undeniably figurative but nevertheless may be figurative. What do we do? Herein lies a good deal of the potential difference between flat or plain interpretation and grammatical-historical interpretation. Flat interpretation acknowledges only obvious figures; grammatical-historical interpretation seeks to acknowledge all figures and allusions. If Ryrie desired to talk about grammatical-historical interpretation, he might better have begun his (i.e., Craven's) sentence with the phrase "the grammatical-historical interpreter" rather than the "literalist."

OTHER STATEMENTS ON LITERALNESS

In contrast to the above quotation, Tan (pp. 29–30) defines grammatical-historical interpretation much more clearly in the first two of the following paragraphs:

> To "interpret" means to explain the original sense of a speaker or writer. To interpret "literally" means to explain the original sense of the speaker or writer according to the normal, customary, and proper usages of words and language. Literal interpretation of the Bible simply means to explain the original sense of the Bible according to the normal and customary usages of its language.
>
> . . . It is proper for a word to have various meanings and senses. However, when a word is used in a given situation, it should normally possess but *one* intended sense of meaning. This is the regular law of linguistic exchange among sensible people.
>
> . . . To "understand" a speaker or writer, one must assume that the speaker or writer is using words normally and without multiple meanings. This is what the literal method of interpretation assumes of God in Scriptural revelation. It believes the Bible to be revelation, not riddle.

Tan has nevertheless biased things seriously toward a flat interpretation by a few turns of phrase. In what Tan says about *words,* the same tendency toward the idea of first-thought meaning may still be at work. In the second paragraph Tan might better have said that in any one occurrence of a word in a piece of text, the word will have only one intended sense *unless the context activates more than one sense.* We have seen in the analysis of Isaiah 27:2–4 that some contexts can activate more than one meaning simultaneously. The word "battle," for instance, in Isaiah 27:4 evokes the idea of both a battle against personal enemies that the Lord might undertake on behalf of Israel (this is the main point) and a metaphorical battle that a gardener might have against briers and thorns. The full impact of the passage depends on the possibility of both of these senses. Similarly "thorns" and "briers" are used in the extended figure involving the vineyard to stand for personal enemies. But they have the power also to evoke a memory of Eden, with its absence of literal thorns and briers. Hence the total impact of the words "thorns" and "briers" depends on the simultaneous presence of a metaphorical and a literal connection.

In fact most metaphors depend for their success on a simultaneous presence of two or more planes of meaning (cf., e.g., Black, pp. 25–47). Hence Tan's third paragraph, if left as it stands, virtually eliminates the possibility of metaphors. Tan presumably did not intend this result. But he fell into a very one-sided statement.

Tan (p. 132) can be even more explicit than he is above.

> Normal human communication demands the fundamental principle that what is being spoken or written be predominantly nonfigurative. A. B. Davidson is happily correct when he says: "This I consider the first [!] principle in prophetic interpretation—to read the prophet literally—to assume [!] that the literal meaning is *his* meaning—that he is moving among realities, not symbols, among concrete things like people, not among abstractions like *our* Church, world, etc."

Tan says that communication is "predominantly nonfigurative." Of course there must be nonfigurative uses of words, against the background of which figurative uses arise. Moreover the language learner typically acquires a sense for the meaning of words by seeing them used in various literal contexts. In this sense nonfigurative uses of a given word will "predominate." But what does this "predominance" of nonfigurative language amount to? It is a predominance within the *total* number of utterances ever heard by the average user of the language. This sort of predominance is quite compatible with the possibility that even very long discourses might be wholly figurative. For instance, Jesus' parables and John Bunyan's allegories are figurative all the way through.

SOME GLOBAL FACTORS IN INTERPRETATION

Moreover Tan's statement does not seem to take into account the possibility that a whole story may be *globally* figurative, without there being any one word or words that are uniquely figurative. Some of the parables of Jesus approach this kind of story. For example the parable of the lost sheep in Luke 15:4–6, taken simply as a story in itself, contains little figurative language. Few of its individual words are used in an obviously figurative way. But in its context in Luke, it is obvious that the story as a whole functions as an extended metaphor relating two planes of meaning. That is, it relates the "husbandry" plane, concerning a shepherd and his sheep, to the "salvation" plane, concerning leaders of God's people and the people.

Now how do we know whether biblical prophecy is like a plodding history writer, or like John Bunyan, or like parables, or like something else? Whether or not biblical prophecy is predominantly or exclusively figurative or nonfigurative ought not to be something "assumed," on the basis of a supposed "fundamental principle" of communication. It ought to be determined by looking at prophecy both in its actual content and its historical context (grammatical-historical interpretation). To make pronouncements beforehand as Tan and Davidson do is to bias the question immediately in the direction of flat interpretation or plain interpretation or both.

Davidson's statement has still another problem, this time relating to the Israel/church distinction. His statement contrasts "reality" with "symbol," "concrete things" with "abstractions." "People" are reckoned as concrete things whereas "our church" and "world" are reckoned as abstractions. But isn't our church one kind of "people"? It looks very much as if the fundamental distinction between heaven and earth is at work here. The church is reckoned as heavenly, and so as somehow not real, not "concrete," whereas other peoples are earthly and hence concrete. Where is such a question-begging contrast coming from? Literalness is almost being made to function as a code word for the classic dispensationalist doctrine that construes the distinction between Israel and the church as a distinction between earth and heaven.

Some may think that I am being too hard on Ryrie, Tan, and Davidson. Are they really begging the important questions? Are they really slanting the case in favor of flat interpretation? Or are they just being imprecise? Maybe they are just imprecise, but the particular way in which they are being imprecise does not help to delineate the issues separating dispensationalist from nondispensationalist hermeneutics. Rather it confuses them.

And this happens in the very context where they are trying to set forth the distinctiveness of dispensationalist approach to hermeneutics over against other approaches!

We may illustrate the problem in still another way. Let us ask ourselves whether Ryrie's or Tan's statements help us to know when and how to find a typological meaning when we are working with a particular Old Testament historical or legal text. Ryrie explicitly allows that there are types. Tan would presumably do so too, though his statement denying multiple meanings for words would seem to exclude it. But both men are so general that they do not tell us about the crucial role of context (both immediate and more distant) in determining whether there is a symbolic or allusive meaning and in determining how far the allusions belonging to such meaning extend. Their vagueness leaves us with the question of whether it is legitimate to apply typological techniques to prophecy as well as history. Scofield says no. But Ryrie and Tan do not immediately distinguish history and prophecy. Hence it would seem that, in principle, they allow typological techniques in both history and prophecy or else in neither.

Over against this conclusion Tan's quote (p. 132) from Davidson, with its pointed exclusion of the church, apparently forbids the use of typological techniques with prophecy. Perhaps Tan is operating with a general principle that is vague enough so that it can be interpreted at one point (historical texts) as allowing a good deal of allusiveness, yet interpreted at another point (prophecy) as minimizing any such possible allusiveness. In that case his general principle would be ambiguous between grammatical-historical interpretation, flat interpretation, plain interpretation, and perhaps still other types of interpretation.

One final quotation may illustrate the problem. Feinberg (p. 46) criticizes M. J. Wyngaarden, a writer he describes as believing "that even in Old Testament times those Old Testament Scriptures [many passages appealed to by Wyngaarden] had to be understood as embodying latent and incipient spiritualization." In rejecting this position Feinberg says:

How those portions *were* understood in Old Testament times, one need not be informed; it is a matter of common knowledge and open to the careful investigation of all. They were taken only and solely as literal.

What does Feinberg mean by "literal" here? He, along with other dispensationalists, assures us that he does freely recognize that there is figurative language in the Bible. So "literal" cannot mean "having no figures of speech." In spite of Feinberg's strong language, "only and solely as literal," he does not mean "no figures." Hence "literal" does not mean first-thought interpretation. Does it connote simply "grammatical-historical interpretation"? In this context evidently not, because then Feinberg's statements would come close to being a triviality. Both Feinberg and Wyngaarden agree that grammatical-historical interpretation is important. The point at issue with Wyngaarden is whether grammatical-historical interpretation does or does not include some spiritualization. Wyngaarden claims that it does. Feinberg claims that it does not. Feinberg distinguishes his position from Wyngaarden using the word "literal." Hence "literal" here corresponds very closely to what I have described as flat interpretation. If I understand him correctly, Feinberg uses the word "literal" precisely in order to assert that grammatical-historical interpretation, in the particular case of Old Testament writings, coincides in its results with what I have called flat interpretation. The original audience was supposed to understand the writings in a flat manner, and hence grammatical-historical interpretation reproduces this flatness.

Now let us suppose that we have understood Feinberg correctly. His claim is exceedingly important. It may be close to the heart of the hermeneutical disputes. But Feinberg does not defend his view. He says merely that his view is "a matter of common knowledge." Unfortunately this knowledge is not "common" to me. I would like the matter to be discussed at some length, not just assumed. Hence I will take up the question in chapters 10 and 11.

In the meantime what is literal interpretation? It is a confusing term, capable of being used to beg many of the questions at stake in the interpretation of the Bible. We had best not use the phrase but rather speak of grammatical-historical interpretation. The word "literal" could still be retained in discussing the meaning of particular words or particular sentences. In that case it would be the opposite of figurative. It would do roughly the same job as my phrase "first-thought meaning."

10
INTERPRETIVE VIEWPOINT IN OLD TESTAMENT ISRAEL

Let us now reflect on how grammatical-historical interpretation will proceed when applied to the Old Testament in general and to Old Testament prophecy in particular. Grammatical-historical interpretation in its narrowest focus asks what human authors meant by what they wrote. But it is not mere psychological speculation about what was going on in the author's mind. It does not make unfounded guesses that the author somehow "must have meant such-and-such" even though the intended audience would have no clue. Rather grammatical-historical interpretation disciplines itself to pay attention to what the author actually *expressed*. It could also be characterized as being concerned with what the author's intended readers would be justified in understanding the text to mean. The latter formulation in terms of readers has the advantage that it forces us to avoid speculation about the author's mind and confine ourselves to what the author actually wrote. Human readers, however, are not infallible. In particular, we are not concerned simply with any meaning that some reader may subjectively read into the text. We want to know what meaning readers are *justified* in finding in the text.

Whichever way we formulate the matter, grammatical-historical interpretation deals with what a passage says against the background of its original time and culture, bearing in mind the purposes of the human author.

ACTUAL INTERPRETATIONS BY
PRE-CHRISTIAN AUDIENCES

Grammatical-historical interpretation, then, focuses on the time when the book was written. We cannot, however, definitely settle an issue over the interpretation of (say) Micah by simply appealing to what Israelites in Micah's time understood Micah to mean. Some of them might be mistaken, through sin or hardness of heart. Moreover, most of the time we do not even have very much information about Israelite understanding of Old Testament passages when they were written. It is hard to know what Feinberg means when he says (p. 46):

> How those [many previously listed] portions *were* understood in Old Testament times, one need not be informed; it is a matter of common knowledge and open to the careful investigation of all. They were taken only and solely as literal.

Of course from the Old Testament's own record of some responses to oral divine words, and occasionally responses to written words, one can tell something about how the respondents understood them. For instance, what happened when God gave commands? Those who responded with immediate, straightforward obedience showed that they understood the commands to have a straightforward meaning. Perhaps the obedient Israelites interpreted God's commands flatly. But perhaps they saw additional implications or allusions beyond the straightforward response. There is often nothing to prove the matter one way or the other, unless we assume that all Israelites were more or less prone to flat interpretation.

The most elaborate evidence we have of general audience interpretation in pre-Christian times comes from the intertestamental period. Does Feinberg have this in mind? Probably not. At any rate it would not support his conclusions. The hermeneutical responses were quite varied. Some individual interpretations were flat. Some were produced by highly worked-up imaginations. One has only to look at Philo Judaeus or the Qumran community or Jewish apocalyptic to see imagination at work (cf., e.g., Philo, *Legum allegoriarum;* 1QpHab, 1QpMic; 1 Enoch; cf. Longenecker, pp. 19–50; Patte).

ISRAEL'S HOPE

Now let us turn to the question, not of *actual* interpretation by Old Testament audiences, but of *justified* or *warranted* interpretation. What did the human author actually express in an Old Testament text? What was the original audience justified or warranted in understanding from Old Testament texts? What was expressed in prophetic texts in particular?

I maintain that several factors in Israel's understanding of itself and its understanding of God should have led to an understanding of prophecy that was not flat. At times, of course, particular prophetic texts would have been understood as mainly or wholly nonmetaphorical predictions. But in other cases Israel's own attitude should have been one of open-ended expectation. Israel was to expect fulfillment of some predictive prophecy, without knowing in exactly what way the prediction would be fulfilled. They would not know exactly to what extent a metaphorical expression of the truth was at work.

A simple illustration of this occurs in Isaiah 40:4–5:

> Every valley shall be raised up,
>   every mountain and hill made low;
> the rough ground shall become level,
>   the rugged places a plain.
> And the glory of the LORD will be revealed,
>   and all mankind together will see it.
>   For the mouth of the LORD has spoken.

Nothing in the immediate or the remote context absolutely constrains the original reader to understand the prediction of verse 4 as anything else than a description of topographical changes (changes in the shape of the surface of the ground). A flat interpretation would therefore say that topographical changes are in view. An interpretation in the original historical context based on the principle "literal if possible" would say the same thing. But the situation is more complicated than flat interpretation understands. True, Israelites are not forced to see this prediction as involving anything more than or anything other than topographical changes. But neither are they forced to maintain that there must be such changes, or that such changes are the main point.

For one thing, the immediate context, like much of Isaiah 40–66, is suggesting the theme of a second exodus (cf., e.g.,

Isa. 43:16–21; 51:9–11; 52:12; 63:7–19). The way through the wilderness (40:3) is language describing a way from captivity (earlier Egypt; now Babylon) to the Promised Land. The language of topographical changes may, then, be a metaphorical expression to indicate the completeness of the preparation involved when God himself comes in the midst of his people.

Secondly, Isaiah 2:1–18 has already used similar language about leveling processes to indicate the exaltation of God and the humiliation of human pride. The Scofield Reference Bible remarks on Isaiah 2:2: "A mountain, in Scripture symbolism, means a kingdom (Dan. 2.35; Rev. 13.1, with Rev. 17.9–11)." Scofield's remark is certainly not flat interpretation. Nor is it strictly grammatical-historical interpretation, since it relies on passages of the Bible not yet written at the time that Isaiah was written. Yet to the sensitive (not the flat) reader of Isaiah 2:12–18, the main point concerns pride and humility, honor and dishonor, exaltation and humiliation, not topographical changes.

Now let us go back to Isaiah 40:3–5. By its choice of metaphorical language, Isaiah 40:3–5 gives us something less "exact" than a prosaic, chroniclelike description of the future. But it gains something in ability to weave together the themes of human pride being brought low, the second exodus, and the cosmic scope of God's final redemption. The godly Israelite reader would know the main point. The Lord will come in a spectacular second exodus, dealing with the pride of man. Whether there are topographical changes, and how far this second exodus will correspond to the first, the passage does not say clearly. This expression of hope will be filled out and become more specific when fulfillment actually takes place. For instance, we know more clearly, in the light of the fulfillment with John the Baptist, that repentance was one primary aspect of the Lord's dealing with the pride of man as alluded to in Isaiah 40:4.

Now let us return to the general question of interpreting prophecy. Old Testament prophecies for the "latter days" do not find their center in the people of Israel pure and simple. Nor is their center in the transformation of the land of Palestine, pure and simple. Rather the deepest roots of their expectations are found in the coming of the Lord. "In the desert prepare the way for the LORD" (Isa. 40:3). "And the glory of the LORD will be revealed" (v. 5). "Say to the towns of Judah, 'Here is your

God!' " (v. 9). "See, the Sovereign LORD comes with power, and his arm rules for him" (v. 10). "[The messengers] say to Zion, 'Your God reigns!' " (52:7). One could multiply passages. The coming of God, the appearing of God in his glory, cannot but imply transformation of the people of God. As at the Exodus and Sinai, so in the future, the coming of God means both judgment and salvation. And the coming of God implies transformation of the land, because wherever the Lord appears becomes holy ground (cf. Exod. 3:5). No wonder, then, that prophecy speaks so much about the people of God and transformation of their land. These things are not isolated from the coming of God. The spectacular transformation of created things exhibits and reflects the overwhelmingly great character of God himself and his revelation of himself in the latter days.

But if the transformations of people and land are determined in their character by the coming of God himself, God is still the deepest center of prophetic expectation. Can an Israelite predict in detail what the coming of God will mean? It does not mean flat interpretation. It means an interpretation over which God himself is the ultimate interpreter. Even Moses saw only God's "back" (Exod. 33:23). To have God revealed in full glory to the whole world (Isa. 40:5) means something so spectacular that the Israelite should be reserved about what is metaphorical, and in what way it is metaphorical.

ISRAEL AS A KINGDOM OF PRIESTS

Israel's self-understanding, in particular, would have affected the way in which it read prophecies about its future. How was Israel supposed to understand itself? Israel as a nation and a people was told by God that its own center of gravity was not in simple biological or ethnic bounds but in its relationship to God. Israel was a people marked out as distinct by bearing the name of God (Num. 6:24–27) and by God's dwelling in its midst (Num. 14:14). The whole nation was to be "a kingdom of priests and a holy nation" (Exod. 19:6). As priests the people were to serve God in holiness (Lev. 19:2) and perform a special, prominent role in bringing the knowledge of God to all the other nations of the world (Gen. 12:3; Deut. 4:6–8).

How, then, was Israel supposed to understand its own priestly role? It was to do so by observing the very concrete model given to it in the Aaronic priesthood. The Aaronic priests (and subordinately the Levites) were, of course, priests in a very special sense. Israel as a whole did not have the same status as did the descendants of Aaron. It is true that the whole community was holy, in a lower sense of holiness (Exod. 31:13). But such holiness did not justify Korah's attempt to level the distinction between priests and people (Num. 16–17). The Aaronic priests were holy in a unique sense. Yet precisely in their uniqueness the Aaronic priests set before the people a model for what they all were to be on a less intensive level.

Aaron then was a model for Israel. But Aaron himself was modeled after something still deeper. The instructions for the tabernacle were to "make them according to the pattern shown you on the mountain" (Exod. 25:40). The tabernacle was a holy place, made after the pattern of heaven, the supremely holy dwelling place of God (1 Kings 8:27, 30, 34, 36, 39). The ministry of the tabernacle also was presumably modeled after heavenly ministry. One recalls the ministry of the angels who are continually in the presence of God, and of Moses with whom God spoke "face to face" (Num. 12:8). Aaron, of course, could not stand before God in his own person. He had to have special holy clothing, or else he would die (Exod. 28:38, 43). Moreover, several of the items and arrangements of the clothing corresponded at least vaguely to the tabernacle itself. The blue, the gold, the rings, the plate marked "Holy to the LORD" were all reminiscent of aspects of the tabernacle (cf. Kline, *Images*, pp. 42–47). Aaron the priest was modeled after a heavenly pattern.

Thus the full pattern for Israel's priesthood had levels of depth. Israel as a whole was priest; Aaron was priest; in God's heavenly original there was the ultimate priesthood. We summarize the relations in Diagram 10.1.

Israel's role as a kingdom of priests therefore possessed symbolic significance. This significance does not at all mean that Israel's priesthood was merely symbolic or merely something of illustrative or pedagogical value. It was not merely an illusion, reflecting the real priestly reality in heaven. It was substantial; it was "real"—on the level that the Israelites could take it, and on the level appropriate to the preliminary character of God's deliverance and his revelation at this point. The true *God,* not merely a surrogate for God, was really present with Israel. And his presence meant their consecration as priests. Yet God was not present in the way and with the intensity that he is present at the coming of Jesus Christ. His presence with Israel was preliminary and "shadowy" in comparison to that.

Diagram 10.1

Israel's Understanding of Its Priestly Existence

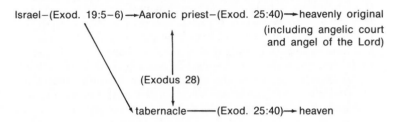

Israel–(Exod. 19:5–6) ⟶ Aaronic priest–(Exod. 25:40)⟶ heavenly original

(including angelic court
and angel of the Lord)

(Exodus 28)

tabernacle———(Exod. 25:40)⟶ heaven

The latter days mentioned in the prophets are that broad eschatological era when the glory of God is revealed on earth (Isa. 40:5; 60:2–3; Zech. 2:5). The glory of God was formerly confined to heaven and subordinately appeared in order to fill the Holy of Holies in the tabernacle and the temple. But eschatologically God will come to earth in his majesty. In those days the heavenly reality will supersede the earthly symbolic reflection. The heavenly original will fill and transform what was shadow. Hence those days imply a revision also in the Aaronic priesthood (Ps. 110:4), and by implication a revision of the law, which is bound up with the priesthood (Heb. 7:12). But more than that, they imply a revision in the existence of Israel itself, since it is constituted as a kingdom of priests (cf. Isa. 66:18–24). Since the existence of Israel itself has symbolic and heavenly overtones from the beginning, the fulfillment of prophecy encompasses these same overtones. The eschatological time is the time when the symbolic overtones in the very nature of Israel itself are transformed into reality.

Consider now what this symbolic dimension meant for Israel's perception of the nature of the land of Palestine. The land belonged to God (Lev. 25:23). It was not to be desecrated by unclean practices (Lev. 20:22–24; Deut. 21:23). In an extended sense the land itself was holy, the dwelling place of God. As a holy land it was modeled after God's rule over his heavenly dwelling, but it also illustrated what God would do to all the earth in the latter days. God's kingdom would come to earth as it was (in Old Testament times) in heaven. The land of

Palestine was also analogous to Eden (Isa. 51:3). It pointed back to what Adam failed to do. Adam's dominion over Eden (the starting point for rule over the whole earth) was ruined by the Fall. Israel was granted dominion over a "new Eden." This dominion over Palestine in turn anticipated the full dominion that was to be restored by the "seed of the woman," one born to be the "last Adam" (1 Cor. 15:45).

These connections imply that it is a violation of grammatical-historical interpretation to read prophecy flat. It is even a violation to read Israel's history flat. The history of Israel has some symbolic overtones derived from the symbolic dimension in Israel's own existence as a kingdom of priests. But eschatological prophecy is the point at which these symbolic overtones are bound to be emphasized and come out into the open, since that is the time of transition from the preliminary to the final.

These symbolic overtones include almost everything that has in the past been classified as typology, and more besides. In fact Israel's existence was so saturated with incipient typology that it is hard for us, who live in the light of the fulfillment, to appreciate the Israelite situation. In a certain sense it is impossible. We cannot forget what we have learned of Christ. But I would say this: Israel could on the one hand know much through a dim sense of symbolic overtones. And simultaneously it could know little because the shadows did not provide all the depth and the richness that the reality provides. A good deal would be known tacitly rather than by explicit, rationally articulated means.[1]

Now one more point should be observed about the eschatological expectations of Old Testament Israel. The "latter days," but not before, is the decisive time when the heavenly reality of God in his glory comes to earth. Therefore prophetic predictions with regard to the *near* future have a character distinct from predictions about the "latter days." In the near future the organized political and social community of Israel continues in more or less a straight line. Predictions, even when they use symbolic and allusive language, can expect to find fulfillment on the symbolic level on which Israel then exists.

---

[1] Martin J. Wyngaarden (pp. 88–135) speaks in this connection of "latent spiritualization" in the Old Testament. I am not altogether satisfied with the way in which he develops his argument, but I believe that the basic idea is sound.

But fulfillment in the "latter days" (eschatological fulfillment in the broad sense of eschatology) is a different matter. There the symbol is superseded by the reality, and hence straight-line reckoning about fulfillments is no longer possible. Preeschatological prophetic fulfillments have a hermeneutically different character than do eschatological fulfillments.

As a simple example we may take the prophecy of Malachi 3:3–4. Malachi prophesied that at a future point the sons of Levi will present right offerings, acceptable to the Lord. If the time in view were preeschatological, it would be natural to assume that this restoration would simply be a restoration of right worship along the lines laid out by Leviticus. But the context of Malachi 3:1–2, even without the use of the special phrase "latter days," appears to be that of overwhelming judgment and overwhelming coming of God. It is the context of the "latter days." In that case it is not so certain that the *form* of the offerings can be expected to remain absolutely the same. Will continual bloody sacrifices still be offered, or (possibly) will offerings be confined to praise and compassion (in analogy with Rom. 12:1; 15:16; Phil. 4:18; Heb. 13:15)? The nature of continual offerings might be changed when a final, definitive sacrifice for purification has taken place (Mal. 3:2; 4:1–3; cf. Heb. 10:1–3).

Some dispensationalists, of course, think on the basis of Ezekiel 44–46 that bloody sacrifices will be renewed in the Millennium. We will not take up the questions about Ezekiel, because that would involve more interpretive disputes. The point is this: for almost any prophetic passage touching on the "latter days," one can claim that it has a perfectly straight-line, obvious kind of fulfillment in the Millennium. Though such interpretation is possible, is it necessarily a genuine implication of the passage in every case? Was the Old Testament hearer obliged to say that the passage must be fulfilled in the most obvious way?

As a second example consider Jeremiah's prophecies. His predictions of disaster in the immediate future (e.g., Jer. 24:1–10) and restoration after exile (e.g., 29:10–14) are fulfilled in a straightforward manner. However Jeremiah also looked toward more distant vistas. He spoke of a more climactic fulfillment, when the whole Mosaic order would be superseded by a covenant of more power, intimacy, and effectiveness—the new covenant (31:31–34). It is obvious that Jeremiah here touched on eschatological realities. In this case interpreting the fulfillment is not as straightforward a matter.

Once again, as we might expect, there are modern disagreements about the passage. Some would see fulfillment as relating exclusively to Jews in the Millennium. But is there a possible alternative? Without denying that there may be a millennial fulfillment, can we say that there is fulfillment in the New Testament era?

When Jesus comes the "latter days" are inaugurated. In particular Jesus at his death inaugurates the new covenant by his blood (Matt. 26:28 and parallels). There is a textual problem about whether the word "new" occurs in any of the accounts of the Last Supper. But the connection is there in any case, because of the mention of covenant, the forgiveness of sins (cf. Jer. 31:34), and the parallel with the inauguration of the Mosaic covenant (cf. Jer. 31:32). Christians celebrate their participation in this covenant by partaking of the Lord's Supper (Luke 22:19; 1 Cor. 11:24–26). It is difficult to escape the conclusion that all Christians, whether or not they are biologically and socially Jews, are participants in the new covenant (cf. Heb. 10:11–22). Because Christ is an Israelite and Christians are in union with Christ, Christians partake of the benefits promised to Israel and Judah in Jeremiah. With whom is the new covenant made? It is made with Israel and Judah. Hence it is made with Christians by virtue of Christ the Israelite. Thus one might say that Israel and Judah themselves undergo a transformation at the first coming of Christ, because Christ is the final, supremely faithful Israelite. Around him all true Israel gathers.

Now many dispensationalists do not fully agree with me in the interpretation of Jeremiah's promise of the new covenant. I do not propose to argue the matter in detail. The important question at this point is not about a specific passage but about principle, a principle of prophetic interpretation. I claim that there is sound, solid, grammatical-historical ground for interpreting eschatological fulfillments of prophecy on a different basis than preeschatological fulfillments. The Israelites of Jeremiah's day should have absorbed (albeit often unconsciously) the earthshaking, transformational character of the eschatological coming of God. It is therefore a move away from grammatical-historical interpretation to insist that (say) the "house of Israel" and the "house of Judah" of Jeremiah 31:31 *must* with dogmatic certainty be interpreted in the most prosaic biological sense, a sense that an Israelite might be likely to apply as a rule of thumb in short-term prediction.

What I am calling for, then, is an increased sense for the fact that in the original (grammatical-historical) context, eschatologically oriented prophecy has built into it extra potential. With respect to eschatology, people in the Old Testament were not in the same position as they were for short-range prophecy. Eschatological prophecy had an open-ended suggestiveness. The exact manner of fulfillment frequently could not be pinned down until the fulfillment came.

ISRAEL AS VASSAL OF THE GREAT KING

Similar conclusions could also be obtained by considering Israel as the servant of the king. God himself was the King over Israel (Deut. 33:5; 1 Sam. 8:7). Israel was the special kingdom of priests over which he ruled by his law (Exod. 19:6). The covenant that God made with Israel is analogous to the suzerainty treaties that Hittite kings made with their vassals (cf. Kline, *Treaty;* id., *Biblical Authority*). Now the fabric of Israel's existence and self-understanding was in fact constructed from the texture of God's covenant with Israel and Israel's servant relation to God the King. The earthly, human king of Israel was to be a reflection of divine justice and divine rule (Deut. 17:14–20; 1 Sam. 8:7). He was like a son of God the Great King (2 Sam. 7:14). As such he also anticipated the final King and Son (Ps. 2:7).

In this connection eschatology or the "latter days" is nothing other than the time when God exerts his kingly power in a climactic way for the salvation of his servant and the establishment of justice in the land (Isa. 52:7). God will become King over all the earth (Zech. 14:9). The arm of his power will be exerted as awesomely as at the Exodus (Isa. 40:10). This manifestation of God's kingship sweeps up within it the human Davidic kingship. God will be shepherd of his people; and David will be shepherd (Ezek. 34:11, 23–24). The action of the one is the action of the other. "The house of David will be like God" (Zech. 12:8). In fact David's son will be the "Mighty God, Everlasting Father, Prince of Peace" (Isa. 9:6).

Thus God's kingship over Israel undergoes decisive transformation and full realization in the eschatological time. Israel's relation to its human kings in the line of David also changes.

Israel itself changes, because it is constituted by its servant relation to the king. In the eschatological time Israel the servant becomes mysteriously identified as the one true servant who will bring God's salvation, and hence his rule, not only to the tribes of Israel, but to all the earth (Isa. 49:3, 6; cf. Acts 13:47). Israel is the people of the king, and the Holy Land is the land of the king's rule. Both pass from symbol to reality in the time of the coming of God's reign.

ISRAEL AS RECIPIENT OF PROPHETIC WORDS: THE GENRE OF TRUE PROPHECY

Finally, similar conclusions can be reached by considering Israel's understanding of the nature and mode of prophecy. In Israel's existence all the prophecies of the prophets were intended to be read against the background of the ministry of Moses. The prophets were spokesmen for the Lord. Moses himself stood as a supreme example of a spokesman for the Lord. Through Moses the Lord also gave some specific instructions to Israel concerning the reception of later prophecy, particularly in Numbers 12:6–8, Deuteronomy 13:1–5, and Deuteronomy 18:14–22. Israel was to test prophets by their adherence to worshiping the Lord alone, and by the failure or success of predictions. Both these presupposed a basic intelligibility to their messages or at least large sections of their messages. On the other hand, Numbers 12:6–8 clearly subordinated the prophets to Moses. Moses surpassed prophets not only in the foundational quality of his role and his message, but in the mode of revelation. With Moses God spoke "face to face" (12:8), in contrast to a more distant or indirect mode of appearance in visions or dreams (12:6). To Moses God spoke "clearly," in contrast to speaking "in riddles." Moses "sees the form of the LORD."

Moses was therefore elevated above the prophets by the degree of closeness that he enjoyed to God. He was closer to the inner reality of God's heavenly presence. The phrases "face to face" and "seeing the form of the LORD" both characterize Moses' experience as one of striking direct and intimate encounter. Yet we know that these apparently strong and absolute expressions are themselves to be understood relatively. Even Moses, in the deepest sense, could only see the "back" of God (Exod. 33:23), and that only in a climactic experience of his life.

If, however, the expressions of Numbers 12:8 are relative, it is easier to understand that the experiences of divine presence by later prophets were in turn relative to those of Moses. Isaiah (Isa. 6:1–8), Ezekiel (Ezek. 1 and other passages), and Daniel (Dan. 7:9–10) saw revelations of the glory of the Lord, revelations of impressive and intensive character. Yet even these experiences were to be subordinated to that of Moses, in view of Numbers 12:6–8.

The clarity and directness of the prophetic message correlates with the clarity and directness of the prophet's relation to God's heavenly presence. To Moses God spoke "clearly and not in riddles" (Num. 12:8). By implication prophets subordinate to Moses spoke in a more riddlelike form characterizing a dream or vision (12:6). Of course God is not giving here a narrow, technically precise characterization of the genre of all later prophetic revelation. Some of it came in dreams or visions (Dan. 7:1; 8:1; Zech. 10:2), but much was not explicitly in this form. Rather, in Numbers 12:6–8 God is giving at least a broad, over-arching characterization of ease of interpretation.

Even a superficial reckoning with Numbers 12:6–8 therefore confronts some of the classic dispensationalists with serious problems. One thinks of Scofield's dictum to the effect that historical Scriptures often have a "spiritual significance" but that in prophetic Scriptures one finds "absolute literalness" (*Scofield Bible Correspondence School,* pp. 45–46). Scofield comes dangerously close to actually reversing the order of Numbers 12:6–8, which is, after all, one of the few explicit statements in the whole Bible on the mode and relative literalness of prophecy.

The challenge of Numbers 12:6–8, however, is deeper than this; for, taken in a larger context, it brings up again the question of the relation of heavenly reality to earthly symbol. Israel was on earth. Since the Fall men have been separated from God's presence. God's "face," God's glory, the reality of God himself in all his attributes, is the center and heartbeat of heaven. What relation did Israel have to this ultimate reality? In Moses' time Moses himself served as mediator (cf. Exod. 20:18–21; Deut. 18:16). The prophets were mediators after the pattern of Moses, though in certain respects inferior to him. Insofar as a prophet was subordinate, Israel might expect that the prophet's message itself would have a veiled or symbolic character. Once again the eschaton is the time of unveiling: unveiling for the nations (Isa. 25:7; 40:5), but also unveiling for Israel (Jer. 31:33–34, contrasting with, say, Isa. 6:9–10).

Until the time of the eschaton, Israel's own existence was ordered by the structures of Mosaic legislation. Hence short-term prophetic pronouncements conforming to the structure of Moses might be expected to find more direct or straight-line fulfillment. The fulfillment is bound to change character when a final prophet arises, one even greater than Moses (Acts 3:22–23).

The above considerations on the nature of prophecy and the mode of prophetic revelation therefore tally with conclusions that Israel could have reached by reflection on its existence as a kingdom of priests and as vassal of the Great King.

11
THE CHALLENGE OF TYPOLOGY

In the previous chapter I have argued that Israel's social and political structures, and even its own existence, had symbolic significance. Especially at the time of Moses, when Israel was organized into a nation, its social structures and character were defined by reference to God himself, his promises, and his glorious dwelling in heaven. The symbolic significance of elements in Mosaic legislation was therefore a "vertical" significance. The various arrangements pointed to God, his character, his plans, and his heaven. But the significance could simultaneously be horizontal. The spiritual realities to which the symbols pointed vertically were to be revealed fully on earth at the time of the eschatological coming of God in his glory. Hence the symbols have a forward-pointing character.

Now we wish to ask how classic dispensationalists have dealt with this symbolic aspect of Old Testament revelation.

DISPENSATIONALIST APPROACHES TO TYPOLOGY

Dispensationalists have known about typology and studied it. They have viewed typology as something that we as New Testament Christians could find in the Old Testament. But most of the time dispensationalists have said very little about the grammatical-historical basis on which New Testament typologizing rests. It has almost appeared that there was nothing in the Old Testament itself, understood on its own, that encouraged any symbolic reflection. Thus New Testament typology has been isolated from the Old Testament symbolic overtones that were already there in Old Testament times.

Now such an approach, used in the past, harmonized very well with Scofield's dichotomous approach to hermeneutics. I do not know whether anyone worked out the logical relations in detail, but it could have been argued that the Old Testament was to be read on two levels. On the one hand, the Old Testament as directed to Israel was intended to be quite prosaic. Symbolic meanings to the tabernacle, the sacrifices, the lives of the patriarchs, the kingship, the life of David, and so on, could be ignored, perhaps should be ignored, by the Israelite. On the other hand, the Old Testament was intended to produce a rich symbolic meaning when related to the church.

Such an approach, however, has become more and more problematic as emphasis was placed on the significance of literal interpretation. Any sort of twofold approach like Scofield's must begin with the assumption of a sharp distinction between two parallel purposes for Israel and the church. If such an assumption just stands by itself, it seems too arbitrary. How do we define "literal" interpretation so that it represents an attractive ideal? The most obvious way would seem to be to make it identical with grammatical-historical interpretation.

Interesting things, however, happen in the confrontation of grammatical-historical interpretation with typology. What does grammatical-historical interpretation do with the Old Testament tabernacle, the sacrifice of Isaac, the life of David, and so on? At least two responses are possible.

On the one hand, one could claim that grammatical-historical interpretation finds no symbolic overtones, or only a minimum of such overtones, in such passages. But this conclusion would be in tension with what the New Testament itself as well as dispensationalist interpreters have done with many aspects of Old Testament historical revelation.

On the other hand, one could say that grammatical-historical interpretation uncovers many symbolic significances in the Old Testament, and that these are right in line with the use that is later made of them in the New Testament. This second alternative is close to my own point of view.

But then the symbolic and typological significances do not disappear when we go over to Old Testament prophecy. Old Testament prophecy is written against the background of Mosaic revelation. If the sacrifices, temple, land, priesthood, and kingship have symbolic significance in Mosaic times, that significance still clings to them when the same themes are mentioned or alluded to in prophecy. In fact, if anything, it will be increased and filled out as the later revelation of the prophets throws light on certain things that may have been in relative obscurity before.

Thus grammatical-historical interpretation, constrained as it is to interpret the prophets against the background of Moses, will go ahead and introduce the symbolic and typological element directly into prophetic utterances about the future. Such a procedure runs counter to Scofield's rigid separation between Old Testament history and prophecy (pp. 22–27). Many modern dispensationalists might nevertheless reconcile themselves to it. They might say, "Old Testament history points to actual ('literal') events and institutions. The symbolic overtones do not cancel out the reality of the events. The same thing happens with prophecy. Prophecy of future things may have both symbolic overtones and straightforward ('literal') fulfillment."

Such an admission by dispensationalists is a significant step forward because it opens the way for vigorous use of Old Testament prophecy in secondary application to the church age. Dispensationalists can still retain literal fulfillments in more or less the form that they had before, but the symbolic overtones of Old Testament history contain typological lessons about us as the church. Similarly the symbolic overtones of prophecy will have implications for us, even if they do not amount to fulfillment.

Having gone this far, however, dispensationalists will have to ask themselves again what fulfillment of prophecy really amounts to. As I have argued, many Old Testament prophecies, though they may have partial fulfillments in the immediate future, anticipate a great and climactic time of fulfillment in the "latter days." At that time the glory of the Lord is definitely revealed and that which is partial and shadowy about Old Testament revelation will be superseded by that which is final and real. Such prophecies are eschatological (having to do with last things) in the broadest sense.

Can we expect eschatological prophecies to operate in exactly the same way as Old Testament histories and institutions? Old Testament histories and institutions, when they involve symbolic, typological overtones, have two dimensions: the symbol itself, and what the symbol symbolizes. Moreover, the symbols do not merely symbolize some timeless spiritual

113

truth. They are not merely vertically oriented. They also point forward in time, at least indirectly, to the same period that is the concern of eschatological prophecy. The two dimensionality is bound up with the fact that Old Testament revelation is preliminary and shadowy in character.

Eschatological prophecy may indeed have the same two dimensions: the symbol in itself, and what the symbol symbolizes. But the time of fulfillment of the eschatological prophecy is the time of climactic revelation. Hence it may well be that at that future time the symbol is superseded by the reality and no longer needs a separate historical realization alongside the reality.

THE TEMPLE AS A TYPE

We may take as an example the temple: the temple of Solomon, the postexilic temple built under Zerubbabel, the temple envisioned in Ezekiel 40–48, and prophecies of the Messiah as temple builder (Zech. 6:12–13). Everyone agrees that the temple is a symbolic, typologicial institution within the bounds of the Old Testament. It is the house of God, symbolizing God's dwelling with human beings. It is modeled after God's dwelling in heaven (Exod. 25:40; 1 Kings 8:29–30). It is a "copy and shadow" of heavenly things (Heb. 8:5). It points "vertically" to God's dwelling in heaven, but it also points forward to the eschatological time when God's dwelling with men will be fully realized.

All Christians would surely agree that Christ's own body is the temple of God (John 2:21; cf. 1:14) and that the church corporately and Christians individually are temples of the Holy Spirit (1 Cor. 3:16; 6:19; Eph. 2:21).

The question now is whether or not the church and Christians are related to a prophecy like that in Zechariah 6:12–13. First of all notice that Christ himself is related to Zechariah 6:12–13. The resurrection of Christ alluded to in John 2:21 is surely part of the fulfillment of Zechariah 6:12–13, because all the promises of God find fulfillment in Christ (2 Cor. 1:20). Now what about Christians? They are raised with Christ (Eph. 2:6); and Christ himself, who is the temple of God, is dwelling in them (Rom. 8:10). That is the sense in which Christians are a temple. Hence, how can we avoid saying that Christians also are part of the fulfillment of the temple-building prophecy of Zechariah 6:12–13?

Consider now the *type* of fulfillment that takes place in the New Testament. In the New Testament era, do we now need a second dimension of symbolism, a temple of material stones? In the Old Testament there were two dimensions, "literal" (temple of stone) and typological-spiritual (the spiritual reality of God's communing with human beings, now realized in the Resurrection and the sending of the Holy Spirit). If there were two dimensions then, should not there be two dimensions now? But that reaction overlooks the theme of the Book of Hebrews. According to Hebrews that which is shadowy (temple of stone) can be "abolished" when it is superseded by the perfect (Heb. 10:9).

Of course the New Testament era itself does not contain the fullest and richest possible realization of God's promises. That fullness comes in the New Jerusalem, in the new heaven and the new earth. In that situation there remains a material, earthly component. Those who are saved are not then disembodied spirits but people with resurrection bodies dwelling in a city that is simultaneously a Holy of Holies, a temple. We shall consider that fact in greater detail in the next chapter.

For the moment it is sufficient that we appreciate some of the challenges that are introduced by the interpretation of symbolic and typological overtones in the Old Testament. Dispensationalists readily agree that these types foreshadow truths concerning Christ and believers in the New Testament. So types are a natural starting point for a discussion with dispensationalists. Since grammatical-historical interpretation will find the same symbolic, typological significance within prophecy, it shows how prophecy also has an organically unified relation to New Testament believers. Typological relations cannot merely be dismissed as a secondary application. The major weakness of classic dispensationalist interpretive theory, at this point, has been the neglecting of the integration of typological interpretation with grammatical-historical interpretation.

A LIMIT TO GRAMMATICAL-HISTORICAL INTERPRETATION

One more difficulty arises in relation to typology. As I argued in the previous chapter, the significance of a type is not *fully* discernible until the time of fulfillment. The type means a

115

good deal at the time, but it is open-ended. One can anticipate in a vague, general way how fulfillment might come, but the details remain in obscurity. When the fulfillment does come, it throws additional light on the significance of the original symbolism.

In other words, one must compare later Scripture to earlier Scripture to understand everything. Such comparison, though it should not undermine or contradict grammatical-historical interpretation, goes beyond its bounds. It takes account of information *not* available in the original historical and cultural context. Hence grammatical-historical interpretation is not enough. It is not all there is to interpretation. True, grammatical-historical interpretation exercises a vital role in bringing controls and refinements to our understanding of particular texts. But we must also undertake to relate those texts forward to further revelation that they anticipate and prepare for.

The influence of further revelation on grammatical-historical interpretation is important because dispensationalist statements about interpretation have almost always omitted it. In fact dispensationalists have frequently rejected nondispensationalist interpretation on the ground that it is "reading the New Testament back into the Old Testament." That way of putting it makes it sound bad, as if the Old Testament does not really support that "reading back." And sometimes the dispensationalists' concerns are well taken: some people's "reading back" has virtually wiped out the influence of grammatical-historical interpretation of the Old Testament.

Let us, however, not escape the difficulties too easily. Dispensationalists themselves do something very like "reading back" when they use typology. They do it also when they form a prophetic system that depends on an integrated interpretation of texts from many different parts of the Bible. All interpreters are bound to strive for integration when they reckon with the fact that the Bible has one divine Author; they must expect a unified and self-consistent message from beginning to end.

Hence I want to appeal to dispensationalists to do two things: (1) to develop a conception of grammatical-historical interpretation that takes seriously symbolic and typological overtones of both Old Testament history and Old Testament prophecy; (2) to be willing to enrich the results of grammatical-historical interpretation with insights that derive only from considering earlier and later Scriptures together. And they must learn to do the latter, not only when it is a matter of typology within Old Testament historical passages, but also when it is a matter of typological or allusive material within Old Testament *prophetic* passages.

Some modified dispensationalists no doubt are already considering earlier and later Scriptures together, since one can do so and still maintain that in the future millennial period there will be relatively straightforward fulfillments of most eschatological prophecies. For me, however, a more important question is whether we are able to affirm that here and there we have fulfillment of prophecy in Christians and in the church. The question of the church has been a point of contention in the past. Further reflection on problems with typology may therefore help to bring us together.

12
HEBREWS 12:22–24

Previously I argued that the Book of Hebrews is the single most important text to consider in a discussion of dispensationalism. More than any other part of the Bible, it reflects explicitly and at length on the crucial question of the relation of the Old Testament to the New Testament. Moreover the Book of Hebrews contains the most explicit discussion of the views on typology that I have developed in the previous chapter.

Unfortunately to discuss the Book of Hebrews as a whole would take too long. I would therefore like to concentrate on a single passage, Hebrews 12:22–24. This passage has not received much attention in dispensationalist debates. By itself I do not suppose that it is capable of settling the debates, but it is of considerable value because of the way it speaks of Christian participation in the heritage of "Mount Zion" and "Jerusalem." Hence I think it may help dispensationalists to loosen up the rigidity that has sometimes characterized the affirmations concerning separate parallel destinies for the church and Israel and concerning the nonfulfillment of prophecy in the church. Perhaps precisely because it has not received much attention yet, it will be a fruitful starting point for some fresh developments.

FULFILLMENT OF MOUNT ZION AND JERUSALEM

Our central concern is the significance of the mention of Mount Zion and heavenly Jerusalem in Hebrews 12:22. What motivates the author of Hebrews to speak in this way concerning Christian privileges? In particular does Hebrews mean to imply that we can speak of Christians coming to Mount Zion as fulfillment of Old Testament prophetic passages like Isaiah 60:14 and Micah 4:1–2?

Mount Zion and Jerusalem have religious significance in the Old Testament primarily because they are the place where the temple of God was built, by God's own direction. Because of their close relation to the temple, they share in the typology that we associate with the temple.

In the Book of Hebrews much is made of the fact that the tabernacle (or temple) on earth is a copy and shadow of God's heavenly dwelling. When Christ came he introduced a "better sacrifice" that brought cleansing to the heavenly original (Heb. 9:13–14, 23). Christ gives us access into the presence of God in heaven (Heb. 10:19–20). Mount Zion and heavenly Jerusalem in Hebrews 12:22 must likewise be the heavenly originals of which the Mount Zion and Jerusalem in the Old Testament were "copies and shadows."

Many dispensationalists (classic dispensationalists as well as modified dispensationalists) would agree with me up to this point. In the past they have had no trouble seeing typological significance in Old Testament historical passages about Mount Zion and Jerusalem. But dispensationalists may have hesitancy about further steps that I suggest. To begin with, the appearance of the antitype of a type is very like the fulfillment of a prophecy. For example Christ's sacrifice, according to the whole Book of Hebrews, is the antitype of Old Testament animal sacrifices, which were types pointing forward to it. Christ's sacrifice is the endpoint, the finished product, to which Old Testament historical sacrifices pointed. Christ's sacrifice is also the fulfillment of prophecies of a perfect sacrifice, not only Isaiah 53, but the phrase of Daniel 9:24: "to atone for wickedness."

Can we draw an analogy between the situation concerning sacrifices and the situation concerning Jerusalem? The heavenly Jerusalem in Hebrews 12 exists by virtue of the presence of Christ as high priest with his sprinkled blood (Heb. 12:24). Hence it would appear to be the antitype to which the Old Testament historical Holy City, Jerusalem, pointed as a type. Therefore we may also expect that it is simultaneously the fulfillment of prophecies about a perfect, restored Jerusalem

(Isa. 60:14; Mic. 4:1–2). According to my arguments in the previous chapter, this is by no means a violation of grammatical-historical interpretation. Grammatical-historical interpretation, having discerned some of the symbolic significance of sacrifice, temple, and city in the Old Testament, would also see symbolic (typological) significance in prophetic material concerning Jerusalem.

ABRAHAM'S HOPE

We can arrive at a similar result by a route more acceptable to dispensationalists. Let us lay aside for the moment the question of whether we want to speak of anything within the New Testament era as fulfillment. There are nevertheless Old Testament prophecies concerning a heightened glory, wealth, and purity to Mount Zion, to Jerusalem, and, indeed, to Palestine as a whole. These prophecies fill out and deepen the foundational promises made to Abraham concerning his inheritance of the land.

What then did Abraham hope for on the basis of God's promises? Hebrews asserts that Abraham was "looking forward to the city with foundations, whose architect and builder is God" (11:10). A few verses later Hebrews explains further. Abraham was a sojourner who did not inherit the promised country in his own lifetime. "They [Abraham and his descendants] were longing for a better country—a heavenly one. Therefore God is not ashamed to be called their God, for he has prepared a city for them" (v. 16). Abraham himself, therefore, understood the promise as involving entering into possession of a heavenly Jerusalem mentioned in Hebrews 12:22. Moreover Abraham even now belongs to the city, since he is included among the "spirits of righteous men made perfect" mentioned in Hebrews 12:23.

Hence Hebrews 12 shows that there is, within this age, a fulfillment of the promise made to Abraham. It is not the final endpoint or most extensive realization of fulfillment: that will be later. But it is nevertheless fulfillment, fulfillment that has come to Abraham and the patriarchs themselves. But what about Jewish Christians? Do they presently share in Abraham's inheritance? They "have come to Mount Zion, to the heavenly Jerusalem" (v. 22). That is, they have come to live in the very city that Abraham was looking for in fulfillment of promise.

Jewish Christians have not become *less* Abraham's children by believing in Christ. They have not somehow been disinherited precisely because they have imitated Abraham's faith! Hence their presence is also an aspect of fulfillment of the promise to Abraham.

Next, what about Gentile Christians? Are they able to come to Mount Zion? Surely they are, because under the gospel they have equal access to the Father with Jewish Christians (Eph. 2:18–19). They share in the blessing to Abraham. This conclusion is exactly in accord with the promise to Abraham: "All peoples on earth will be blessed through you" (Gen. 12:3). The apostle Paul develops this very argument in Galatians 3:7–9, 26–4:7. Thus the coming of Gentile Christians to Mount Zion in Hebrews 12:22 is a fulfillment of the promise to Abraham.

Some dispensationalists might say, "This is a beautiful application, but not actually a *fulfillment.*" As we have seen, that reply is always available within the dispensationalist system. But it looks as if we are then disagreeing with Abraham's own understanding. Hebrews says that Abraham was expecting this city, and the promise to Abraham says that Gentiles are to be included in the blessing. Abraham himself would have seen it as fulfillment, and who are we to say otherwise?

Dispensationalists nevertheless have an important point to make. This fulfillment in Hebrews 12:22 is "a" fulfillment, but not the greatest, broadest, most climactic realization of the promises to Abraham. Such fulfillment is still future. We err if we minimize this. On the other hand, some (fortunately not all) dispensationalists have erred in the reverse direction by a point-blank denial of fulfillment in Gentile Christians.

THE NEW JERUSALEM IN REVELATION

All premillennialists believe that the promises to Abraham will find fulfillment in a more complete way in the millennial period, following the return of Christ. Let us assume for the sake of the argument that they are right. Yet even that fulfillment is not the whole story. The promises are still to be fulfilled in the new heaven and the new earth of Revelation 21:1–22:5. This final fulfillment is important because of its links with Hebrews 12:22.

Already there is a difficulty. Dispensationalists disagree

among themselves concerning the nature of the material in Revelation 21:1–22:5. Almost everyone agrees that Revelation 21:1–7 describes the "eternal state," but Revelation 21:9–22:5 is variously interpreted (cf. Pentecost, pp. 563–83). Some dispensationalists think 21:9–22:5 also describes the eternal state. Others think it describes the Millennium. Pentecost prefers to see it as a combination: the heavenly Jerusalem of Revelation 21:9–22:5 will be the eternal abode of all saints, but it is described as it exists during the millennial period.

Everyone agrees that there is a close relation between Revelation 21:9–22:5 and Revelation 21:1–7. Therefore unless there are factors pointing the other way, grammatical-historical interpretation would conclude that both describe the same situation. If we keep firmly in mind that the eternal state includes a new *earth,* the apparently earthy character of some aspects of 21:9–22:5 is quite in harmony with the eternal state. Even the mention of the healing of the nations in Revelation 22:2 goes little beyond the mention in Revelation 21:4 of wiping all tears away. Both are a counterpoint to the suffering and imperfections in the main part of the Book of Revelation. In fact there are no good arguments against Revelation 21:9–22:5 being the eternal state, unless one begins with dogmatic assumptions that the eternal state *must* have few features in common with the Millennium.

It is not even necessary, however, to establish that Revelation 21:9–22:5 describes the eternal state, provided we at least admit that the Jerusalem mentioned there is an earlier stage of the Jerusalem coming down from heaven in the eternal state (Rev. 21:1–7). All must admit this much, because the heavenly Jerusalem is indestructible (Heb. 12:28; see Pentecost, p. 580). Whichever option we use in interpreting Revelation 21:9–22:5, the New Jerusalem described in both 21:1–7 and 21:9–22:5 is in fundamental continuity with the heavenly Jerusalem of Hebrews.

Of course the New Jerusalem of Revelation 21 describes the situation at a later point in time than does Hebrews. Between now (Hebrews) and then (Revelation) we know that there is an advance in revelation and in the working out of God's purposes. But nevertheless there is a continuity between the two. In favor of this continuity notice the following: (1) the designation as "Jerusalem" shows a close connection; (2) the New Jerusalem of Revelation 21 "comes down from heaven," the location of the Jerusalem of Hebrews 12:22, which will not pass away even with the shaking of heaven and earth; (3) Hebrews tells us that Abraham was looking for the heavenly Jerusalem (11:10, 16), and within Revelation Abraham's destiny must be in the New Jerusalem; hence the two are the same; (4) dispensationalist commentators themselves find no trouble in identifying the two (Kent, p. 272; Newell, p. 426; Pentecost, p. 579; Walvoord, *Millennial Kingdom,* p. 326).

Since Christians share in Abraham's inheritance of the heavenly city now, they will share in it then also. It is legitimate to distinguish Jew and Gentile as peoples with two separate origins. But their destiny (if they come to trust in God's promises) is the same: they share in the inheritance of the New Jerusalem coming down from heaven. Hence the idea of two parallel destinies, heavenly and earthly, falls away.

THE NEW EARTH

Some dispensationalists might object that our argument does not pay attention to the proper distinction between heaven and earth. Christians participate in the heavenly Jerusalem, but Israel must yet have an earthly fulfillment in an earthly Jerusalem in the Millennium.

In Revelation 21, however, the New Jerusalem comes down from heaven *to earth.* The earthly fulfillment of Old Testament prophecy finds its climax in Revelation 21–22. Abraham certainly participates in this earthly fulfillment. Other Jews will participate. Jewish Christians are not disinherited from their Jewish heritage just because they imitate Abraham's faith. Hence they participate. But then Gentile Christians must also participate, because they are coheirs by virtue of union with Christ the Jew (Eph. 3:6). In Revelation 21–22, therefore, a strict isolation between heavenly and earthly "destinies" is not possible. In the new earth Christians are related to the *earthly* realization of the Abrahamic promises. Thus since they enjoy membership in the heavenly Jerusalem, they are experiencing the first installment in the Abrahamic promises.

If some of us reject the idea of Christian participation in fulfillment, it is not because we insist on literal fulfillment. The Jerusalem in Revelation 21:1–22:5 can be interpreted as literally as one wishes, and it says nothing against Christian participation. If we deny Christian participation, it is rather because of wanting to maintain a strict separation of heavenly and earthly destinies. The claim of separate *destinies* says something more and different from the (correct) claim that the peoples have separate origins. The idea of separate destinies in fact has come into systematized theories without having any textual support at all.

Some dispensationalists are now admitting that the idea of strict compartmentalization of heaven and earth is a mistake. Kenneth Barker (p. 12) says:

> Strictly speaking it is also incorrect to call Israel God's earthly people and the Church God's heavenly people, since in the eternal state we will all live together sharing in the blessings of the New Jerusalem and the new earth. . . .

> So, then, there is a greater unity or integration in God's grand design and in his overall purpose and comprehensive program for this earth and its people than many dispensationalists have been willing to acknowledge. In the past some of us have not been able to see the forest for the trees. We have compartmentalized too much.

THE IMPORTANCE OF HEBREWS 12:22

In summary, then, the passage in Revelation 21–22 is valuable to our discussion because its emphasis on the new earth shows that the final destiny of Christians and of Israel is similar. This is already a challenge to the most rigid forms of dispensationalism, which emphasize the idea of two distinct destinies, as different as heaven and earth. Hebrews 12 is valuable because it shows that Christians already experience a foretaste of the fulfillment of Revelation 21–22, and hence they are related to Old Testament "Jewish" promises.

Finally, Hebrews 12 is also valuable because of the way that it relates heaven and earth. Classic dispensationalism construed heaven and earth simply as two separate spheres in which the two separate destinies of the church and Israel were realized. But Hebrews 12 sees the two as related to one another in terms of shadow and reality, historical anticipation and fulfillment. It therefore presses dispensationalists away from a vertical alignment of church and Israel running on parallel tracks and towards a historical, typological alignment of church and Israel as belonging to successive historical stages.

One should note, however, that these arguments based on Hebrews 12:22–24 have the most weight against more rigid forms of dispensationalism that deny absolutely that any Old Testament prophecies are fulfilled in Christians and the church. Erich Sauer and others do acknowledge fulfillment in the church, though they see the most literal fulfillment in the Millennium. Such positions have already digested some of the primary implications of Hebrews 12:22–24. Further reflection about the unified nature of fulfillment for Abraham and for Christians in the Millennium might lead to an even greater move toward seeing a fundamental unity in destiny and inheritance of the people of God in all ages.

13
THE FULFILLMENT
OF ISRAEL IN CHRIST

The central distinctive of classic dispensationalism is the principle of the parallel-but-separate destinies of Israel and the church. Israel and the church are two peoples of God, earthly and heavenly. As we now approach this principle from the standpoint of systematic theology, we need to remember that many present-day dispensationalists have modified the principle of parallel destinies. The criticism of this chapter may therefore not apply to them.

For those who do hold to the principle of two destinies, the most incisive direct challenge to this principle arises from reflection on the biblical teaching on fulfillment in Christ.

BECOMING HEIRS TO
OLD TESTAMENT PROMISES

I have already mentioned briefly (pp. 42–43) the argument for the church's connection with the prophetic promises of the Old Testament. The argument is strongest if one does not bluntly and simplistically assert that the church is a straight-line continuation of Israel. Rather one proceeds by way of Christ himself as the center point of fulfillment of the promises. Christ is an Israelite in the fullest sense. In fact, though all Israel be rejected for unfaithfulness (Hos. 1:9), yet Christ would remain as the ultimate faithful Israelite, the ultimate "remnant" (cf. Isa. 6:11–13; 11:1). Hence as 2 Corinthians 1:20 says, "No matter how many promises God has made, they are 'Yes' in Christ." The question then remains, "What does union with Jesus Christ bring to Christians?" The church receives the complete fullness of God's blessing through Christ (Eph. 1:23; Col. 2:10), including being made coheirs with Christ (Rom. 8:17). That is to say that we inherit what he inherits. We are sons of Abraham because he is (Gal. 3:29). In being united to him, we possess the whole world (1 Cor. 3:21–23).

This argument can be further reinforced by reflections about the nature of union with Christ. Being united to Christ is an intimate, personal, experiential concern, but it is not only that. Union with Christ has a corporate dimension to it. The church is a corporate organism formed by the union of its members to Christ and therefore also to one another. But Paul extends our sights even further by pointing out an analogy between Christ and Adam (Rom. 5:12–21; cf. 1 Cor. 15:45–49). The fall of Adam is overcome and reversed by the One who is fully a man, a man standing at the head of a new humanity. The old humanity (all who are united to Adam) fell into sin, damnation, disinheritance, and disfellowship through the one man Adam. The new humanity receives righteousness, salvation, inheritance, and fellowship with God through the "last Adam," Jesus Christ. The people of God are, in the end, those whom Jesus Christ represents and ministers to as their Head. Above we talked about the question of inheriting promises, but inheritance is one part of a larger picture: the picture of a new humanity. The new humanity receives righteousness, salvation, inheritance, and fellowship in counterpoint to the fall of Adam.

The unity of the people of God is secured by the unity of the one Head, Jesus Christ. We have already set this forth briefly at an earlier point (pp. 42–43). But now we are ready to see the dilemma that this presents to dispensationalists of the classic type. Though some dispensationalists have made unguarded statements, dispensationalists want to maintain that there is only one way of salvation. In all dispensations salvation is by the grace of God, appropriated by faith in his promises. Suppose that we try to spell out in greater depth and detail what this way of salvation is. It is by the grace of God. But what does "grace" mean? How is it possible for a righteous God to save the unrighteous? The grace of God is bound up with the substitutionary work of Jesus Christ. Grace was given already in the Old Testament, before Christ completed his work, but it was given in anticipation of that work (Rom. 3:25).

What does faith mean? Faith is not faith in faith, or faith in a vacuum, but faith in God's promises, his covenantal commitments pointing forward to the day when salvation will be fully accomplished in Jesus Christ. When the time of accomplishment comes, we see that the work of Jesus Christ is the work of the last Adam. And we find that the unity of the one work of salvation implies a unity of the new humanity that is saved in Christ. Hence the conclusion is not far behind that there is only one people of God. With regard to this point, Fuller (*Hermeneutics of Dispensationalism,* p. 178) expresses the dilemma clearly: "While they [dispensationalists] wish to think of salvation as always administered in the same way [through faith in God's Word, and by the blood], yet they do not wish to carry this idea out to the logical conclusion that all saved persons will have the same status [Israel and the church alike]."

REASONING FROM SALVATION TO CORPORATE UNITY IN JESUS CHRIST

The dilemma can be further illustrated by laying out a series of gradual steps, starting from aspects of salvation and ending with aspects of corporate unity. At each step we emphasize that union with Christ is the one and only means of blessing. At the beginning, when we consider aspects of salvation, dispensationalists wish to agree with the emphasis on unity in order to maintain the unity of the way of salvation. At the end, when we consider aspects of corporate unity, they find themselves having to break down their idea of two peoples of God.

We can begin, then, with justification as an aspect of salvation. Those who are saved are justified by faith. Moreover, justification is ultimately a substitutionary act. Christ's righteousness counts for us, and our sins are laid on Christ. We are "justified in Christ" (Gal. 2:17). Next, the power of transformed lives also comes from Christ. We are "sanctified in Christ Jesus" (1 Cor. 1:2). Spiritual fruit flows from abiding in Christ (John 15). This language of union with Christ is very similar to the language of Galatians 3. There, in the context of justification, Paul says that we are "all sons of God through faith in Christ Jesus" (Gal. 3:26). Then he goes on to say that we are "all one in Christ Jesus" (v. 28). And then we can go to the expressions with even more pointed corporate emphasis: we are reconciled "in this one body" (Eph. 2:16) we are "in Christ . . . one body" (Rom. 12:5), "the body of Christ" (1 Cor. 12:27; Eph. 1:23).

Union with Christ is an organic relationship that includes in a tightly interwoven way both salvation (including just-ification, adoption, and sanctification) and corporate unity. One cannot be saved except in union with Christ, and union with Christ means being part of one people of God.

Dispensationalists, however, are quick to observe that the people of God in the Old Testament did not enjoy union with Christ in the same way that we do. Christ had not yet become incarnate; he had not died; he had not risen again; he had not sent the Holy Spirit. Then how were people saved in the Old Testament? They were saved by the anticipation of these things and by a kind of preliminary "working backward" of their effects—else there is just no salvation at all in the Old Testament. Dispensationalists and nondispensationalists alike who maintain the unity of the way of salvation must admit this conclusion in some way or other. But then the difference between Israel and the church is fundamentally the difference between the people of God *before* and *after* the coming of Christ to accomplish salvation.

The implication can be seen in another way by asking about the future of people of Jewish descent. How are these people to be saved and come into their inheritance? Now that Christ has accomplished his work, salvation is no longer a matter of types and shadows, of anticipations or foretastes. Salvation is by union with Christ and by no other way. That salvation, whether now or in the Millennium, constitutes Jews and Gentiles as "members" of Christ. They are corporately one as a new humanity. Hence one cannot now contemplate splitting apart the new humanity that is under one head, under Christ. One cannot contemplate a Millennium in which salvation is in union with one man, the last Adam, Jesus Christ, but in which that union is undermined by the distinctiveness of two peoples of God with two inheritances and two destinies, on earth and in heaven.

14
OTHER AREAS FOR POTENTIAL EXPLORATION

Having touched on the points that seem to be of most decisive importance in creating fruitful dialogue with dispensationalists, I want to set forth several other points, some of which I have already mentioned, that invite further exploration. In some cases, at least, they might provide complementary ways of approach.

SUBJECTS YET TO BE EXPLORED

1. The Book of Hebrews provides the most extensive discussion anywhere in the Bible of the interpretation of the Old Testament (see pp. 68–69). Study of the whole Book of Hebrews can be undertaken in an effort to develop interpretive principles affecting the understanding of the Old Testament.
2. Matthew's citations from the Old Testament provide indisputable cases of fulfillment, since he often uses a citation formula "that it might be fulfilled" (see the observations on pp. 53–55). These also, therefore, might provide a starting point for examination of interpretive principles for Old Testament prophecy.
3. Revelation 21:1–22:5, though it does not quote directly from the Old Testament, is filled with Old Testament language and allusions. Discussion might focus on the way Old Testament prophecies are fulfilled in the pictures presented in Revelation 21:1–22:5. This discussion, it seems to me, might influence a dispensationalist

in two ways. First, it might challenge the tendency at least among some dispensationalists to concentrate so much on fulfillments in the Millennium that no attention is given to the consummation as an even greater fulfillment. Second, Revelation 21:1–22:5 integrates heaven and earth. It integrates images applying to the church (Gal. 4:26) and Old Testament prophecy directed to Israel (e.g., Isa. 60:19–22; Ezek. 47). Questions about the unity of one people of God and the nature of literal fulfillment can therefore fruitfully be raised in this context.

POSTSCRIPT TO THE
SECOND EDITION

Since the original publication of *Understanding Dispensationalists* in 1987, we have seen further articulation of modified dispensationalism and one-people-of-God dispensationalism, as I described them in chapter 3. In particular, we may examine the most recent developments in Craig A. Blaising and Darrell L. Bock, eds., *Dispensationalism, Israel and the Church: The Search for Definition* (Grand Rapids: Zondervan, 1992).[1] These developments strengthen the directions that my book mapped out and was intended to promote. They harmonize with what I saw taking place in a smaller way in 1987. Hence, in substance my book is still as relevant now as it was then.

A PHYSICAL KINGDOM

However, now that I have received some responses from dispensationalist readers, I wish to clarify and strengthen three points. The first concerns the expectation of a future "physical kingdom on earth for Israel," as expounded by Paul S. Karleen.[2] Many dispensationalists, even of a modified sort, think that this expectation of a physical kingdom constitutes a major bone of contention and an irreducible line of division separating them from covenant theologians.

But let us be careful to define and understand what sort of "physical kingdom on earth" we envision. I agree with Anthony A. Hoekema in emphasizing that the consummation includes a new *earth* as well as a new heaven (Rev.

---

[1]We should also note the continued discussions under the auspices of the Dispensational Study Group, which meets yearly in connection with the annual national meeting of the Evangelical Theological Society. In November, 1989, the group focused discussion on my book, and the results were published in *Grace Theological Journal* 10 (1989): 123–64.

In addition, the major material from the Dispensational Study Group in 1990 appears in *Grace Theological Journal* 11 (1990): 137–69.

[2]The words come from Paul S. Karleen's review and response, "Understanding Covenant Theologians: A Study in Presuppositions," *Grace Theological Journal* 10 (1989): 132. See my comments in Poythress, "Response to Paul S. Karleen's Paper 'Understanding Covenant Theologians,'" *Grace Theological Journal* 10 (1989): 148–49.

21:1).[3] Moreover, I understand this new earth to be a transfiguration and renewal of the old earth, just as the resurrection body will be a transfiguration of the old body (Phil.
3:21). This new earth will be physical and material, just as
Jesus' resurrection body is palpable flesh and bones (Luke
24:39). The transfigured body will indeed be "spiritual" in the
sense of 1 Corinthians 15:44–46. But this "Spiritual" character of the new involves being filled with the Holy Spirit
and structured and empowered by him. Spiritual does not
mean ethereal, in contrast to material, but rather eschatological in contrast to the "natural" order, the preeschatological
order. The new earth, then, will be physical and material in
nature. In this new earth all of redeemed Israel will enjoy
kingdom dominion. As Revelation 5:10 says, ". . . and they
will reign on the earth." And Matthew 5:5 promises,
"Blessed are the meek, for they will inherit the earth." In
short, I *do* believe in a future "physical kingdom on earth,"
and I think that it is a weighty mistake to believe otherwise.

Doubtless dispensationalists would still not be satisfied
with my view. What they have in mind is a *millennial* kingdom for Israel, a kingdom on *this* old earth, not the new
earth. Many (but not all)[4] of them think that a radical distinction must be made at this point, because they still envision the new earth of the consummation as entirely other
than and unrelated to this present earth. Only the millennial
earth remains in substantial continuity with this present
earth. But here miscommunication is a real danger. Their
"new earth" is not the same as my new earth. Instead, my
new earth is practically indistinguishable from their millennial
earth. In fact, I think that it is even better than they imagine. All evil is gone.

THE FUTURE ROLE OF JEWISH BELIEVERS

The second major point as issue concerns the fact that
this future kingdom is "for Israel." Here if anywhere is the

[3]Hoekema, *The Bible and the Future* (Grand Rapids: Eerdmans, 1979)
[4]David L. Turner, "The New Jerusalem in Revelation 21:1–22:5: Consummation of a Biblical Continuum," in Blaising and Bock, eds., *Dispensationalism,
Israel and the Church,* pp. 264–92, helpfully emphasizes the continuities between the millennium and the consummation.

place where even modified dispensationalists and progressive dispensationalists endeavor to make a distinction between themselves and nondispensational premillennialists.

What does it mean that the kingdom is "for Israel"? Along with most covenant theologians, I think that believing Jews and believing Gentiles together inherit the promises made to Abraham and to David. Dispensationalists, on the other hand, are concerned to maintain that faithful Jews, as a distinctive ethnic group and a nation, have a distinctive role in the millennial kingdom. Then what *type* of distinctive role belongs to faithful Jews in the kingdom, after the Second Coming of Christ?

Once again, we must be careful to understand what various people actually have in mind. Within a covenantal position such as mine, it is possible vigorously to assert the ethnic diversity of people groups within the kingdom of God. Within the church today there are various ethnic groups: Jewish, Gypsy, Polish, Lithuanian, Quechuan, Chinese, Burmese, Bantu, Comanche, and so on. In New Testament times, Gentile Christians and Jewish Christians each retained distinctive customs and ethnic practices. Gentiles were not required to become Jews, nor were Jews required to become Gentiles (they could, for instance, continue to circumcise their children and observe Mosaic customs, Acts 21:21).

There is, then, every reason to believe that this wonderful diversity displays something of the glory of the body of Christ. As such, it continues to appear in transfigured form after the Second Coming (Rev. 21:24). Ethnic, social, and even geographical diversity among peoples are quite compatible with the spiritual unity of the body of Christ.

Thus, within covenantal theology, emphasis on the unity of *one* people of God in Christ is quite compatible with a recognition of ethnic diversity. Conversely, almost all dispensationalists nowadays freely acknowledge that there is only one way of salvation in Christ. By virtue of union with Christ, Jews and Gentiles alike enjoy equal *spiritual* privileges in Christ.

Thus the present-day differences between covenant theologians and dispensationalists are not necessarily so great as they might seem. Covenantal theologians are able to acknowledge some of the significant ethnic distinctiveness of Jewish believers; dispensationalists are able to acknowledge some of the significant privileges common to all groups.

Nevertheless, important differences do remain. Dispensationalists believe in a future distinctive *religious* status and role for believing ethnic Jews as a group; covenant theologians do not. To move forward we must, I think, focus the discussion clearly on this issue.

We may further clarify what the key issue is by stating what it is not. We do not question whether believing Jews may retain their ethnic, social, geographical, or other colorful distinctives. Certainly they may, and such differences may even form a positive contribution to the diversity in the body of Christ. Second, we do not question whether believing Jews will inherit the land and the kingdom promises of the Old Testament. Certainly they will. In other words, we do not question whether the future "physical kingdom on earth" is "for Israel."[5]

The issue is whether it is for believing Gentiles also. Do believing Jews at some future point have some distinctive priestly privileges or religious blessings *from which believing Gentiles are excluded?* Does the phrase "for Israel" in actuality mean "for Israel and *not* for Gentiles"? Or does it mean, "for Israel and for believing Gentiles also, who inherit such blessings through union with Christ"? Classic dispensationalism insists on the former meaning. Covenant theology insists on the latter.

Hence, the discussion is not clarified when people merely ask whether Jews have some distinctive role in the future kingdom. It all depends on what *kind* of distinctive role is in view. Ethnic distinctiveness, yes; distinctive religious or priestly privileges or blessings from which others are excluded, no.

Dispensationalists find themselves in a dilemma at this point, as I indicated in chapter 13. They wish to affirm the unity of one way of salvation in Christ. But then they run up against the arguments of Paul in Galatians 3, where he shows how the reality of justification through faith in Christ leads inexorably to the conclusion that Gentiles have the same religious privileges as Jewish believers. Since Paul's argument is based on central realities concerning the way of salvation in Christ, it must hold for the future kingdom af-

---

[5]Though it might better be said that believing Israel comes into the kingdom. See Bruce K. Waltke, "A Response," in Blaising and Bock, eds., *Dispensationalism, Israel and the Church,* p. 352.

ter the Second Coming. At that time, believing Jews will indeed enjoy the priestly and kingly privileges of the kingdom of David. But there is no biblical basis for saying that believing Gentiles will *not* share equally in these privileges. Moreover, such exclusion of the Gentiles contradicts Galatians 3 and is therefore antigospel. Hence, Gentiles are included rather than excluded.

When the Gentiles are religiously included, however, the most important feature distinguishing dispensationalism from covenantal premillennialism disappears, and it is no longer meaningful to use the term *dispensationalism* to label the position so taken.[6]

[6]"If one envisions a Jewish millennium in which the kingdom will be restored to ethnic Israel in the land, the term *dispensationalism* will still be useful. If ethnic Israel's role is only its remnant status on a permanent equality with the Gentiles in the one true people of God with no distinctive role in the land beyond the Parousia, then the term *dispensationalism* is misleading and ought to be dropped" (ibid., p. 354).

Let us be more specific about the implications. Theoretically, one might imagine a situation where, in the future kingdom, Jewish Christians live predominantly in the land of Palestine, whereas Gentile Christians live predominantly elsewhere. Such geographical distinctiveness does not in and of itself create a problem. However, dispensationalists want to find particular religious significance in one special land, the land of Palestine, as distinct from other lands. Canaan undeniably had such significance in the Old Testament period, because, I would argue, it typified the inheritance of the world in Christ (Rom. 4:13; Heb. 11:16). But suppose now that we postulate that in the future some space or land is peculiarly holy or peculiarly the fulfillment of God's promise. Then Gentiles must have equal participation in this inheritance, else we violate Galatians 3.

It will not do merely to say with classic dispensationalism that Gentile and Jewish Christians inherit heaven as distinct from earth. With this position one disinherits Jewish Christians from the earthly aspect of the blessing. One thus flies in the face of all the Old Testament promises that dispensationalists count most precious.

Nor will it do to say that Galatians is talking only about "spiritual" blessings in some narrow sense. For it would then still be true (according to a dispensationalist understanding) that Jewish Christians, but *not* Gentile Christians, would in the future inherit the material aspect of blessing. Now, the Gentiles should be zealous to obtain all the blessings of God that they can. If they are missing out, even on subordinate future "material" blessings, they have grounds to be circumcised and become full-fledged Jews in order not to lack these additional blessings. It is precisely this idea of an additional blessing that Paul resists with all his might.

The danger is not, as dispensationalists think, that covenantal unity automatically disinherits believing Israel (it does not), but rather that dispensationalists illegitimately exclude Gentiles from some of the full privileges that Jews will have in the future through Christ.

No dispensationalist has shown a way to maneuver around the fundamental dilemma: the one way of salvation is through union with Christ. Union with Christ leads to full enjoyment of all blessings, whether we are Jews or Gentiles. The future never undoes what Christ has accomplished. Such are the implications of Galatians 3. Thus Galatians 3 is a rock on which dispensationalist views of the future must break to pieces.

I have personal sympathy and appreciation for the search that progressive dispensationalists have undertaken as they have moved beyond certain features of classic dispensationalism. I am glad to see the moves that they are making, because they seem to me to be expressing biblical truth more faithfully than before. I appreciate also the irenic tone manifested in their work. However, their position is inherently unstable. I do not think that they will find it possible in the long run to create a safe haven theologically between classic dispensationalism and covenantal premillennialism. The forces that their own observations have set in motion will most likely lead to covenantal premillennialism after the pattern of George E. Ladd.

SYMBOLIC DEPTH

Finally, I remain convinced that the area of typology is particularly crucial (chap. 11). Appreciation of the symbolical depth inherent in Old Testament revelation[7] breaks down literalistic (flat) assumptions about the nature of God's communication. Once these assumptions are disposed of, it can be seen that the faithfulness of God to his promises is in harmony with a flexibility about the exact form of fulfillment. The flexibility clears away our inhibitions about giving primacy to the New Testament's instruction about the form of fulfillment.

---

[7]Note that I do not see typology merely as a product of later commentary on earlier events, but as adumbrated by the significance of events even in their original context. The theocentric character of biblical revelation invites us *from the beginning* not to take the route of flat reading.

BIBLIOGRAPHY

For convenience many of the works are classified according to their millennial position: Disp. = dispensational premillennialist; Classic premil = classic or historical premillennialist; Amil = amillennialist; Postmil = postmillennialist.

Allis, Oswald T. *Prophecy and the Church*. Philadelphia: Presbyterian and Reformed, 1945. Amil. A classic against dispensationalism.

Barker, Kenneth L. "False Dichotomies Between the Testaments," *Journal of the Evangelical Theological Society* 25 (1982): 3–16. A moderate dispensationalist (close to classic premil) calls for rapprochement.

Barr, James. *The Semantics of Biblical Language*. London: Oxford University Press, 1961.

Bass, Clarence B. *Backgrounds to Dispensationalism: Its Historical Genesis and Ecclesiastical Implications*. Grand Rapids: Eerdmans, 1960.

Beecher, Willis Judson. *The Prophets and the Promise*. New York: Crowell, 1905.

Berger, Peter L., and Luckmann, Thomas. *The Social Construction of Reality: A Treatise in the Sociology of Knowledge*. London: Penguin, 1967.

Berkhof, Louis. *The Second Coming of Christ*. Grand Rapids: Eerdmans, 1942. Amil.

Black, Max. *Models and Metaphors: Studies in Language and Philosophy*. Ithaca, N.Y.: Cornell University Press, 1962.

Boettner, Loraine. *The Millennium*. Philadelphia: Presbyterian and Reformed, 1958. Postmil. A survey of the major options, antagonistic to dispensationalism.

Chafer, Lewis Sperry. "Dispensationalism," *Bibliotheca Sacra* 93 (1936): 390–449. Disp.

————. *Dispensationalism*. Dallas: Dallas Seminary Press, 1951. Disp.

Cox, William E. *An Examination of Dispensationalism*. Philadelphia: Presbyterian and Reformed, 1971. Amil. Brief, combative.

Darby, John Nelson. *The Collected Writings*. Reprint. Ed. William Kelly. Oak Park, Ill.: Bible Truth Publishers, 1962. Disp. Foundational writings of dispensationalism.

————. *Letters of J. N. D.* Reprint. 3 vols. Sunbury, Pa.: Believers Bookshelf, 1971. Disp.

Dodd, Charles Harold. *According to the Scriptures: The Substructure of New Testament Theology*. London: Nisbet, 1953. Dodd is in the end a modernist. But he is good at laying bare the idea of fulfillment presupposed in New Testament use of the Old.

Dollar, George W. *A History of Fundamentalism in America*. Greenville, S.C.: Bob Jones University Press, 1973. The historical development of American dispensationalism described from a dispensationalist perspective.

Ehlert, Arnold D. *A Bibliographic History of Dispensationalism*. Grand Rapids: Baker, 1965. Disp. Marred by a focus on "dispensations" as redemptive epochs rather than on the distinctives of modern dispensationalism.

Fairbairn, Patrick. *The Interpretation of Prophecy*. Reprint. London: Banner of Truth, 1964. An excellent older work now in reprint.

Feinberg, Charles L. *Millennialism: The Two Major Views. The Premillennial and Amillennial Systems of Biblical Interpretation Analyzed and Compared*. Third and Enlarged Edition. Chicago: Moody, 1980. First and second editions under the title *Premillennialism or Amillennialism?* Disp. A standard dispensational text.

Fish, Stanley E. "Normal Circumstances, Literal Language, Direct Speech Acts, the Ordinary, the Everyday, the Obvious, What Goes Without Saying, and Other Special Cases," *Critical Inquiry* 4 (1978): 625–44. Reprinted in Fish, *Is There a Text in This Class? The Authority of Interpretive Communities*. Cambridge: Harvard University Press, 1980. Pages 268–92. The role of world view and interpretive standards in the determination of meaning.

Fuller, Daniel P. "The Hermeneutics of Dispensationalism." Th.D. dissertation, Northern Baptist Theological Seminary, Chicago, 1957. Classic premil.

————. *Gospel and Law: Contrast or Continuum? The Hermeneutics of Dispensationalism and Covenant Theology*. Grand Rapids: Eerdmans, 1980.

Gaebelein, A. C. *The Prophet Daniel: A Key to the Visions and Prophecies of the Book of Daniel*. New York: Our Hope, 1911. Disp.

Gaffin, Richard B. "Systematic Theology and Biblical Theology," in *The New Testament Student and Theology*. Vol. 3. Ed. John H. Skilton. Philadelphia: Presbyterian and Reformed, 1976. pp. 32–50.

————. *The Centrality of the Resurrection: A Study in Paul's Soteriology*. Grand Rapids: Baker, 1978. Amil.

————. *Perspectives on Pentecost: Studies in New Testament Teaching on the Gifts of the Holy Spirit*. Grand Rapids: Baker, 1979.

Grant, James. *The Plymouth Brethren: Their History and Heresies*. London: W. H. Guest, 1875.

Hendriksen, William. *Israel in Prophecy*. Grand Rapids: Baker, 1974. Amil.

Hoekema, Anthony A. *The Bible and the Future*. Grand Rapids: Eerdmans, 1979. Amil.

Hughes, Philip E. *Interpreting Prophecy*. Grand Rapids: Eerdmans, 1976. A semipopular exposition of covenantal amillennialism.

Jensen, Irving L. *Jensen Bible Study Charts*. Chicago: Moody, 1981. Disp.

Kent, Homer A., Jr. *The Epistle to the Hebrews: A Commentary*. Grand Rapids: Baker, 1972. Disp.

Kline, Meredith G. *Treaty of the Great King: The Covenant Structure of Deuteronomy*. Grand Rapids: Eerdmans, 1963. Amil.
_____. *The Structure of Biblical Authority*. Grand Rapids: Eerdmans, 1972.
_____. "The Covenant of the Seventieth Week," in *The Law and the Prophets*, ed. John H. Skilton. Nutley, N.J.: Presbyterian and Reformed, 1974. Pages 452–69. Amil. A discussion of the key text in Daniel 9.
_____. *Images of the Spirit*. Grand Rapids: Baker, 1980. Old Testament biblical theology, including symbolic overtones of Old Testament institutions.
_____. *Kingdom Prologue I*. South Hamilton, Mass.: Meredith G. Kline, 1981.
Kraus, Clyde Norman. *Dispensationalism in America: Its Rise and Development*. Richmond: Knox, 1958.
Ladd, George E. *Crucial Questions About the Kingdom of God*. Grand Rapids: Eerdmans, 1952. Classic premil.
Lindsey, Hal. *The Late Great Planet Earth*. Grand Rapids: Zondervan, 1970. Popular dispensationalist rapture theory.
Longenecker, Richard N. *Biblical Exegesis in the Apostolic Period*. Grand Rapids: Eerdmans, 1975.
McClain, Alva J. *The Greatness of the Kingdom: An Inductive Study of the Kingdom of God*. Chicago: Moody, 1959. Disp.
Marsden, George M. *Fundamentalism and American Culture: The Shaping of Twentieth-Century Evangelicalism: 1870–1925*. New York and Oxford: Oxford University Press, 1980.
Mauro, Philip. *The Gospel of the Kingdom: With an Examination of Modern Dispensationalism*. Boston: Hamilton Brothers, 1928. Classic premil.
_____. *The Hope of Israel*. Swengel, Pa.: Reiner, 1929.
_____. *The Seventy Weeks and the Great Tribulation: A Study of the Last Two Visions of Daniel, and of the Olivet Discourse of the Lord Jesus Christ*. Revised. Swengel, Pa.: Bible Truth Depot, 1944.
Newell, William R. *Hebrews Verse by Verse*. Chicago: Moody, 1947.
Patte, Daniel. *Early Jewish Hermeneutic in Palestine*. Missoula, Mont.: Scholars, 1975.
Pentecost, J. Dwight. *Things to Come: A Study in Biblical Eschatology*. Findlay, Ohio: Dunham, 1958. Disp. A full working out of details of eschatology.
Pieters, Albertus. *The Seed of Abraham*. Grand Rapids: Zondervan, 1937.
Radmacher, Earl D. "The Current Status of Dispensationalism and Its Eschatology," in *Perspectives on Evangelical Theology*, ed. Kenneth S. Kantzer and Stanley N. Gundry. Grand Rapids: Baker, 1979. Pages 163–76.

Reese, Alexander. *The Approaching Advent of Christ: An Examination of the Teaching of J. N. Darby and His Followers*. London: Marshall Morgan and Scott, n.d. Classic premil.

Ridderbos, Herman N. *Paul and Jesus: Origin and General Character of Paul's Preaching of Christ*. Philadelphia: Presbyterian and Reformed, 1958. Amil.

_____. *The Coming of the Kingdom*. Philadelphia: Presbyterian and Reformed, 1962.

_____. *Paul: An Outline of His Theology*. Grand Rapids: Eerdmans, 1975.

Robertson, O. Palmer. *The Christ of the Covenants*. Grand Rapids: Baker, 1980. Amil.

Ryrie, Charles C. *The Basis of the Premillennial Faith*. New York: Loizeaux Brothers, 1953. Disp.

_____. "The Necessity of Dispensationalism," in *Truth for Today*, ed. John H. Walvoord. Chicago: Moody, 1963. Disp.

_____. *Dispensationalism Today*. Chicago: Moody, 1965. Disp. An introduction to dispensationalism.

Sandeen, Ernest R. *The Roots of Fundamentalism: British and American Millennarianism 1800–1930*. Chicago: University of Chicago Press, 1970.

Sauer, Erich. *The Dawn of World Redemption: A Survey of Historical Revelation in the Old Testament*. Grand Rapids: Eerdmans, 1953. Disp. A moderate form of dispensationalism allowing multiple fulfillments.

_____. *The Triumph of the Crucified: A Survey of Historical Revelation in the New Testament*. Grand Rapids: Eerdmans, 1953. Disp.

_____. *From Eternity to Eternity: An Outline of the Divine Purposes*. Grand Rapids: Eerdmans, 1954. Disp.

Scofield, Cyrus I., Ed. *The New Scofield Reference Bible. The Holy Bible containing the Old and New Testaments. Authorized King James Version*. New York: Oxford, 1967. Disp.

_____. *The Scofield Bible Correspondence School, Course of Study*. 7th ed. 3 vols. No place or publisher is given. Disp. (The title page shows that this edition, unlike some later editions, was actually authored by C. I. Scofield. Moreover the copy in the library of Westminster Theological Seminary, inherited from the library of C. G. Trumbull, has a handwritten appreciation in the front: "To Charles Gallandet Trumbull . . . with the love of The Author." Clearly Scofield claims to be the "author," not merely a final editor.)

_____., Ed. *The Scofield Reference Bible. The Holy Bible containing the Old and New Testaments. Authorized Version*. New and improved edition. New York: Oxford, 1917.

Silva, Moises. *Biblical Words and Their Meaning: An Introduction to Lexical Semantics*. Grand Rapids: Zondervan, 1983.

Tan, Paul Lee. *The Interpretation of Prophecy*. Winona Lake, Ind.: BMH Books, 1974. Disp.

Van Gemeren, Willem A. "Israel as the Hermeneutical Crux in the Interpretation of Prophecy," *Westminster Theological Journal* 45 (1983): 132–44.

_____. "Israel as the Hermeneutical Crux in the Interpretation of Prophecy (II)," *Westminster Theological Journal* 46 (1984): 254–97.

Vos, Geerhardus. *The Teaching of Jesus Concerning the Kingdom of God and the Church*. Reprint. Philadelphia: Presbyterian and Reformed, 1972. Amil.

_____. *The Self-Disclosure of Jesus: The Modern Debate About the Messianic Consciousness*. Reprint. Grand Rapids: Eerdmans, 1954.

_____. *The Pauline Eschatology*. Reprint. Grand Rapids: Eerdmans, 1961. Amil.

_____. *Biblical Theology: Old and New Testaments*. Reprint. Grand Rapids: Eerdmans, 1966.

Walvoord, John F. *The Millennial Kingdom*. Grand Rapids: Dunham, 1959. Disp.

Walvoord, John F., and Zuck, Roy B. *The Bible Knowledge Commentary: An Exposition of the Scriptures by Dallas Seminary Faculty*. Wheaton, Ill.: Victor, 1983.

Wyngaarden, Martin J. *The Future of the Kingdom in Prophecy and Fulfillment: A Study of the Scope of "Spiritualization" in Scripture*. Grand Rapids: Baker, 1934.